THE OLD GREEN ROCKER

To Mother—Christmas—December 25, 1959

That old green rocker must really be wise

With its unseen ears and its unseen eyes.

First, baby Jack was rocked safe in its arms

With you holding tight to protect from harm.

Then blonde-haired Millicent lulled by its beat

With you singing softly—an added treat.

Next, "roly-poly" Pat curled on your knee

To listen to stories and poetry.

Teresa, too, sat on a cool summer night

To listen to crickets in the moonlight.

Yes, that old green rocker must really be wise

With its unseen ears and its unseen eyes.

And in my life, it has helped me so much—

Memories of it to reach out and touch.

So though I may travel to unknown parts,

The old green rocker will stay in my heart.

I love you—Patricia Ann

Caliora Publishing
5403 Crestwood Rd.
Knoxville, TN 37918

Copyright © 2008 by Patricia Combs Oaks

Instead of copying portions of this book, please tell your friends and
family to buy a copy from Patricia at her website:

patoaks.com

First Printing
Edited in Pages 3.0.2
Typeset in Arial Narrow, Helvetica and Times New Roman
by John thomas Oaks

johnthomasoaks.com

Manufactured in Knoxville, TN, USA

This book is because of my family

Tommy (The Best in Every Way)
John thomas
Jason Amos
Misty Michelle
Caleb Travis
Gillian Eliora
Gretta, the Wonder Dog

Thanks also to John thomas
for helping me put this together

Thanks, too, to Greg Moffatt
for sending me fan letters for over twenty years

Introduction

This book is a collection of articles I have written since about 1972.
Some have been published, some have not. I hope that you enjoy
reading them and that some will strike a chord with you
to help you remember happy times in your past.

So pull up a rocker to the fire, read and rock your cares away!

Aunt Billie

She was born Mary Laverna Forester, but because she always followed my grandfather everywhere he went, he called her his little Billie Boy. Hence, she has always been Billie. My Aunt Billie lives in a tiny place called Hubbard Springs, Virginia. There are no stores there—none at all. There isn't even a post office. The valley where she lives is extremely isolated. My cousin Richard and his wife Jeri live next door, which is a real blessing. Her children (Barbara and Joe, Judy and Bill, Jack and Harriet) live out of state, but come often to visit. Her house is three stories high and she drives her car to church each week. She has had that car for as long as I can remember. You may be wondering what is so unusual about any of this and why I am including it in this book. The reason is that my Aunt Billie will be 93 this September (2008)! She looks twenty years younger than that. My grandmother (Billie's mother) was 96 when she died, but she was wrinkled like a little old prune—not my Aunt Billie!

I tell you all of this to introduce you to my aunt, but the real story I want to tell you happened thirty years ago. My mother was dying of cancer. She was given six months to live, and almost six months to the day she went to be with the Lord. My sister and I were taking turns sitting with her. I even had to learn to give her pain shots while she was still home. When she went to the hospital for the last few weeks, the days and nights blended. One of us would stay for 48 hours and then switch. I would come home physically, mentally and emotionally exhausted and fall into bed. About halfway through the hospital stay, my Aunt Billie showed up, suitcase in hand. Now there were three of us keeping watch, so not only was our burden lightened, but our spirits were lifted because our Aunt Billie was there. She was not only taking care of our mother, she was inadvertently taking care of us!

My mother died in the spring of that year and Billie's husband, my Uncle Marshall Giles, came to pick up Aunt Billie and take her home to Virginia to get her clothes for the funeral. On the way up the road, my uncle got sick.

Aunt Billie thought it was food poisoning from a hamburger they had eaten along the way, but it turned out to be a brain tumor in the pituitary gland. It was removed, and for the next nineteen years, Aunt Billie cared for Uncle Marshall. With the master gland gone, several other glands did not function properly, so he had to take thyroid and diabetes medication. Mostly, though, it was cortisone that kept him alive. When he would lose muscle control or verbal ability, he had to be rushed to the emergency room for a shot. There were those who said he would not have lived as long as he did had it not been for the care he received. Although it was extremely difficult for Aunt Billie, especially in the last years, she never faltered in doing her part to save his life.

Uncle Marshall has also since gone to be with the Lord. Aunt Billie continues to be the loving, caring person she has always been. My husband says she has the gift of hospitality. We both love staying in her home. It's one of the few places I feel content besides my own home.

This story is meant to be a tribute to a Proverbs 31 Woman, but even Proverbs 31 doesn't do her justice! Thank you, Aunt Billie!

> **She is a woman of strength and dignity, and has no fear of old age. When she speaks, her words are wise, and kindness is the rule for everything she says. She watches carefully all that goes on throughout her household, and is never lazy. Her children *(and niece!)* stand and bless her; so does her husband! He praises her with these words: "There are many fine people in the world, but you are the best of them all."**
>
> —Proverbs 31: 25-29
> (Living Bible, phrase added by me!)

I love you, Aunt Billie!

> *Aunt Billie recently had a great granddaughter*
> *who is named for my mother, Lila Elizabeth.*

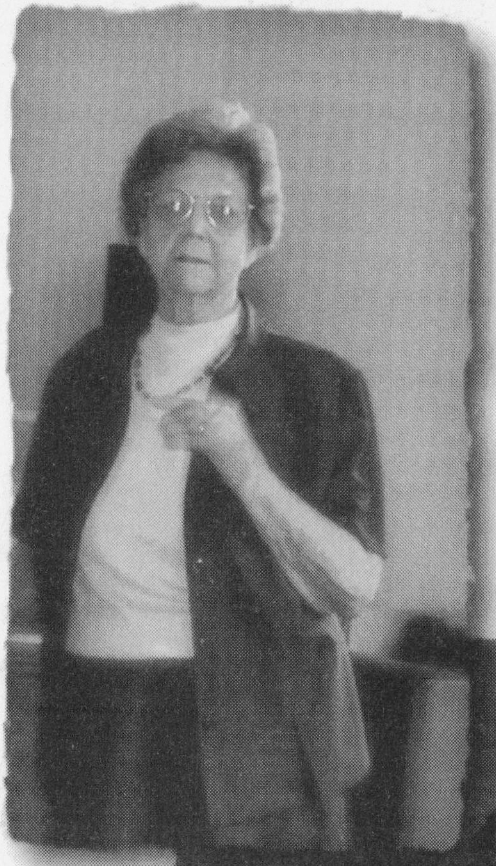

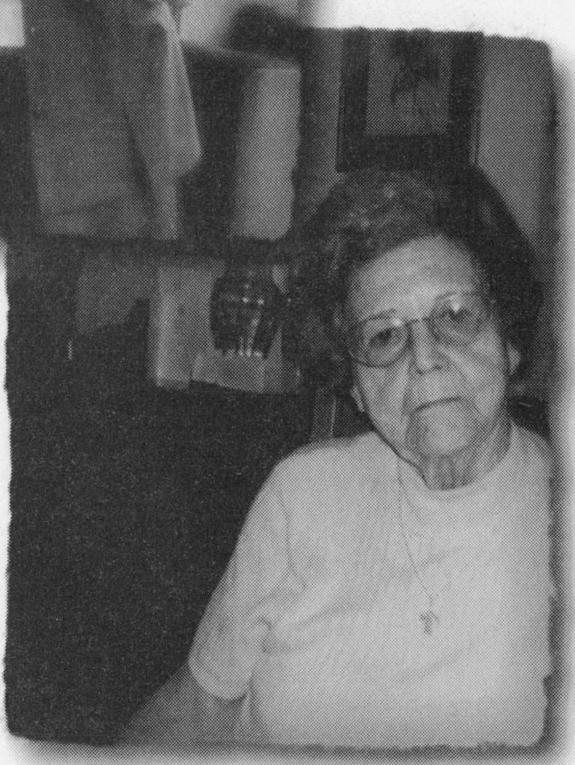

Be a Clown!

As he ran out to the car after school, his eyes were shining! "Tomorrow we get to go to school dressed like clowns!" he cried. As we drove home, he was jumping up and down with excitement. He told me all about how all the children in his class were going to dress like clowns, and how there was going to be a big parade through all the other rooms. I asked him if he was sure that it was tomorrow and he assured me it was.

The next day dawned bright and clear—and so did Jason. He could hardly contain himself (he usually drags in the morning!). I put a pair of pants on him that were too short and a shirt of his daddy's. Then I added a pair of bright, multicolored suspenders and put a red beret on his head. I painted his cheeks and lips bright red and sent him off to school. All day I could picture him in his clown suit and marching in the parade. I could hardly wait to pick him up. Finally, 3:15 came and I drove to school to get him. He ran to the car, eyes sparkling, dimple flashing. "How was it,

Jason? How was your day? Did everyone think you looked good? How was the parade?" My questions tumbled over each other.

"Oh, Mommy," he said, "I forgot! We're not supposed to dress up until tomorrow!"

Well, I laughed until I thought I would fall out of the car. I drove around front to see his teacher, and when she saw me coming, she started laughing, too. "We certainly enjoyed Jason today," she said.

I enjoy Jason every day. He is a joy. Are you? If not, try being a clown. It does not matter if no one else is. You can be! I love this poem:

Laugh and the world laughs with you.

Weep and you weep alone.

This sad old earth

has need of your mirth—

It has tears enough of its own.

—Ella Wheeler Wilcox

Be a clown. The parade is passing you by.

Beans in Your Ears?

My friend Ramona was fuming. "I can't believe anyone could be so rude!" she muttered. "She walked right off and left me in mid-sentence!" I smiled, but I wasn't amused. The same thing had happened to me at a coffee shop a short time before. The host had come over to me and asked a question. Before I could respond, she spied a newcomer and left me to greet her. She never returned. Another time I was at a dinner party in the middle of telling a story that I thought was quite interesting. Obviously no one else thought so. One guest excused himself to go to the bathroom. The attention shifted to him as he left the room and never returned to me. I looked around for someone who was still listening, but no one was. Realizing I was talking to the air, I hushed.

I am sure most of us could recount experiences where we have been made to feel insignificant because we have been unable to hold the attention of our listeners for even a few seconds. Who of us has not experienced talking to someone whose eyes keep shifting around the room as if to say, "I'll endure this until someone more interesting comes along." In such a situation, it's often a relief to the speaker when someone else does come along and provide the inattentive "listener" a means of escape.

What's wrong with a society in which people are so obsessed with their own voices and viewpoints that they see little value in what others have to say? If we do all the talking and seldom listen, won't that make us a little empty? Won't we grow shallow if we continue only to throw out our own thoughts and never receive the ideas of others? What has happened to the ability to listen? Listening is a gift that not many people have. We all would like to be clever-tongued, holding an audience spellbound with our knowledge and wit. Who of us does not like to be the center of attention and want people to think of us as entertaining and fun to be around? I would like to be this way myself. However, because of the experiences I have described, and given the choice between speaking and listening, I much prefer the latter.

There is an old saying that goes:

> **A wise old owl sat in an oak.**
> **The more he heard, the less he spoke.**
> **The less he spoke, the more he heard.**
> **Why can't we be like that old bird?**

Why can't we, indeed? I am sending out a plea and a challenge for listeners—people who will try to develop the art of listening (for it is an art, you know). It takes a very special type of person to be a listener. A listener must not only listen, he must hear. It's like the song where the children sing:

> **Look, Ma, we've got beans in our ears.**

and the mother replies:

> **That's nice, dear, but don't put those beans in your ears.**

People can usually tell if someone is listening with his whole being or if he is just being polite. To be a good listener, a person should be willing and prepared, if need be, to not talk—or at least to not talk very much. You see, a listener listens! David Eubanks is a great example of a good listener. Thank you, David!

Years ago, Taylor Caldwell wrote a book called THE LISTENER. In the story, there was a place where people could go and talk and talk to someone who sat behind a curtain and listened. I won't reveal any more about it except to say that if you are interested in becoming a listener, read this book.

Is anyone listening, or do we all have beans in our ears?

Be Nice

I was going home for my grandbaby Caleb's fourth
birthday. My husband, oldest son and I had been living in
New York City, and I had not seen my youngest son,
daughter-in-law or grandson for two months. I was eager
to get home! The plane sat on LaGuardia's runway for
ninety minutes before takeoff. When we finally started
moving, the pilot said we were seventeenth in line!

My connecting flight was in Pittsburgh and I was afraid I
was going to miss it. When I finally got off the plane in the
B Concourse, I learned I had to go to E, so I started running
through the airport. One of those little carts that I've
secretly always wanted to ride pulled up beside me. The
girl driving it said, "Get on!" So I did. I felt like a big shot
zipping through the airport with her beeping at people to
get out of the way. When I got to my gate, I thanked her
profusely and jumped out, running up to the counter. A
gentleman (he really was!) was standing there. "Slow
down," he said. "You still have twenty minutes left.

You have time to relax and catch your breath."

Then he told me he liked my oak leaf-acorn-patterned sweater and asked if there was any connection to it and my last name. All of a sudden, I felt a great calm and peace come over me. When I went through the gate to get on the plane, the nice man was taking our boarding passes.

"You're a nice person," I said.

"Thank you," he said. "So are you."

What are you? Every day we face circumstances involving other people where we can choose to be nice or hateful. How wonderful we feel when someone is nice to us! What a difference it makes!

Another incident happened at LaGuardia Airport. My husband Tommy had had a heart attack (although we didn't know it at the time). His plane was late and I was waiting at the curb. I always try to avoid driving in New York City, so I was already a nervous wreck. When Tommy didn't show up on time, I started to panic. I knew he was sick, so I was pacing beside my car. A young guard came over and told me he would watch my car if I wanted to go in and check on the plane. How many airport curbside security guards do you know who would do that? At the same time this was happening, my girlfriend Ginger who was supposed to be vacationing in New York was sitting at my apartment trying to arrange a doctor's appointment for Tommy.

I have many stories about people who have been kind to me and made life better. When I come across this goodness in people, it makes me want to reach out and make life better for someone else. I don't want to go through life being a grump and a grouch. I don't want to ignore all the people around me who just might need my help—even if all they need is a smile and a kind word.

So get ready. If you don't think you have any gifts—if you think the Lord may have ignored you in that department—walk out your door and just be nice. That's all.

Thanks for the sweater, Molly!

Big Things in Small Packages

Little Drops of water,

Little grains of sand,

Make the mighty ocean

And the pleasant land;

So the little moments,

Humble though they be,

Make the mighty ages

of Eternity.

—Julia Carney

God often teaches us big lessons in small ways. We may look for His guidance in big things: TV programs, dynamic sermons, how-to books—but all along He might have something else in mind. Much of Jesus' teaching was centered on simple, small incidents such as sowing, reaping, making bread, sewing clothes, and keeping sheep. Here was the greatest teacher ever known to man, but His teachings were presented in "ordinary" packages. I have always been impressed with the list of things God chose to use listed in I Corinthians 1:26-29. Paul starts the list by telling us what God did not use. Not many wise. Not many mighty. Not many noble. What kinds of things does He use? Foolish things—weak things—base things— things which are despised—even things that "are not." Why does He use such things? Paul's answer: "That no man should boast before God" *(v. 29)*

It's easy to forget that God may want to teach us something big in a small way, because the small places frequently appear to be not worth noticing. I once read an article by a leader of a missionary organization who said that they could always find people to write songs, do artwork and preach from a pulpit. The big problem they had was finding anyone willing to sweep the floors, stack boxes or address envelopes. In eight years, the organization had seen nine janitors come and go. The leader commented that it was perplexing that so few individuals could be found who would stay after hours to vacuum carpets and empty wastebaskets. Yet somewhere in that smaller work, it is possible that God had something to teach.

Theresa of Alvia, a famous sixteenth century Spanish believer, once lost her sense of God. She said she found the presence she had lost upstairs walking among the pots and pans.

You never see a small thing coming. Many times you know in advance when a big thing is going to happen—you are going to receive an award—you are going to speak or perform to a stadium filled with thousands—you are invited to a dinner at Tavern on the Green where Gregory Peck and Lauren Bacall are guests (as happened to John thomas!). Usually these big things don't change your life. At the moment those small life-changing things happen, you often don't even realize that your life has been changed. The realization comes later when you look back on the event.

I have recently been trying to cultivate a sensitivity to what God might have to teach in the small places. I am beginning to wonder how many lessons I might have missed, simply because I was not looking for the big lesson in the small way. A couple of lessons I don't think I missed were given to me at (of all places) our local Kmart. The lessons were not given by celebrities. I never even caught the names of the teachers. They were common, everyday people who probably did not even know that they were giving a testimony. God used them, however, to give me some big lessons in a small way. I hope that after reading these two stories, you will agree with me that a visit to your local Kmart can be a life-changing experience—if you have ears to hear and eyes to see, and if you really listen and closely observe.

The Summer Sandals

They were walking in the front door as I was. They were an older couple—rather shriveled looking. She was tiny and had white hair. He was much taller and seemed to tower over her. I just glanced at them and went on into the store. I was in the store about fifteen minutes and thought no more about the couple until I passed the shoe department. She was trying on a pair of dainty, white summer sandals. They were the type of sandals a young teenage girl might wear. She was admiring them on her feet—turning her foot first one way and then another. As I walked on by I heard her ask her husband, "What do you think?" He replied, "They look beautiful."

If their clothing and overall appearance was any indicator, this couple did not have much money—but they had what appeared to be a strong marriage and, best of all, a deep love and respect for each other. In a time when so many marriages seem to be falling apart, I walked away feeling hopeful and encouraged. A strong, happy marriage does not need material wealth, perfect bodies, or any of the things the world tells us every day we need to be happy. I was reminded of that in a powerful way at the Kmart!

Another Kmart Story

I was sitting outside the Kmart waiting on the bus to take me downtown. Waiting on the bus and riding on the bus can be very exciting experiences. Some real "characters" choose the bus for their means of transportation. Of course,

I realize that someone somewhere could just as easily write about what a "character" they observed when they saw me at the Kmart bus stop!

I was doing my usual people-watching and just enjoying the beautiful day God had given me. Suddenly, two elderly, talkative women walked up and sat down on the bench beside me. It was impossible for me not to listen in on their conversation. They were talking about the weather—just chitchat. Then one of the women said to the other, "I'm glad it's nice today. I don't like going to the mall when the weather isn't pretty." The other one agreed with her. Then one of the women asked the other one, "Have you ever been out to West Knoxville where the Cedar Bluff shops and restaurants are?" The other woman replied,
"No, I haven't. I've been wanting to go with some of my girlfriends, but every time I suggest a day, they have hair, dental or doctor appointments, and we never seem to be able to find a day when we can all go together." Then this sweet little lady made the profound statement that

somehow I instinctively knew I had been waiting to hear. She said, "I have heard that you can go there early in the morning, stay all day, have fun and then come home."

For some reason, I thought about that all day long. That night, I told Tommy about it. He thought it was wonderful! In the days that have followed, it has become a philosophy of life for me. Life can be hard, and there are times when things aren't so much fun. I realize that—but life is also meant to be enjoyed. I believe that, and I believe in looking for that enjoyment. God placed us here early in the morning. We're going to stay a while on this earth, so let's have fun while we're here. Then, let's all go home.

I'll be at the bus stop in front of Kmart—want to meet me there?

The Bike Ride

The stories in this book go back over 40 years. As I was trying to sort through my material and decide what I wanted to include, I realized I had not written about one very important event. The following story happened over twenty years ago.

We tried to always do what we said we were going to do. We saved up to buy our whole family bicycles and told our two boys we would go on a bike ride from Elizabethton, Tennessee to Knoxville, Tennessee—a distance of about 125 miles. Finally, the day came. We made a sign for the bicycles that said, "Knoxville or bust!" and started out. Unbeknownst to us, we had picked the hottest two days of the summer! None of us had helmets, so everything from our head down burned! We stopped at a drugstore to get some sunscreen. The owner took one look at us and gave us the sunscreen! He wouldn't take any money for it! We had called ahead to a church in Morristown and asked if we could spend the night in their building. We rolled into Morristown about eleven that night, not realizing that the church was across town! I almost didn't make it. We had been on the road since seven that morning. We slept in the nursery that night. We put crib mattresses on the floor to sleep on. I was so tired I couldn't stop shaking. The muscles in my neck hurt for six months after the trip!

The next day, we headed out again. We had gone about 75 miles the first day, so we had about 50 to go to reach my sister, Teresa's house. We rolled into Knoxville about 2:00 that afternoon, but again, my sister's house was across town! We finally got to her house around 3 or 4:00. I have never been so glad to see someone! She had a huge meal waiting for us, and I don't think I have ever tasted food that good! I will never again say I am "going down" to Knoxville from Elizabethton. It may be south, but it is definitely not down!

Maybe you are wondering why I wanted to write about this. Maybe you are thinking it was no big deal, but my first

reason is to encourage you to do what you say you are
going to do. Second—to have adventures. The trip was
not easy. I was truly miserable most of the time. It seemed
to hurt me worse than Tommy, John thomas and Jason, but
looking back, I remember so many good things. I
remember riding down Highway 107 early the first day—I
remember all the summer smells, sounds and sights. I
remember the boys going ahead of us and just enjoying
watching them. I remember them stopping at a field of
cattle and yelling, "MOO-O-O!" and all the cows running
across the field toward them (no joke—that really
happened!). I remember one big hill that we coasted down
that seemed to go for miles. Every time we go down that
hill in the car, I remember. But most of all, I remember that
we did it. Our family said we were going to do it, and we
did! That feeling of accomplishment did something to our
family. We were closer afterwards than before. I think all
of us felt that there was nothing we couldn't do if we had
each other and the Lord. We still feel that way over twenty
years later.

Bobby

We were with a group of friends on Roan Mountain, a favorite hiking spot close to our house. I was walking with Bobby, a good friend I have known for many years. I was telling him about a funny incident that had recently happened to me. As he always does when you tell him something funny, Bobby threw his head back and gave a long and loud belly laugh. Sometimes when someone tells a story like that, it never seems to be as funny when told secondhand, but Bobby always laughs as if he were there the first time. After he wiped the laugh tears from his eyes, he turned to me and said something so wonderful and profound, I will never forget it. He said, "You know the good thing about us, Pat? You didn't have to be there!"

That's the way it is with good friends.

The Chewing Gum Lady

She lives alone in a tiny trailer within walking distance of the church. She is always there, rain or shine. If someone offers her a ride home at night, she whips out her trusty little flashlight. She declines the offer, thanks them anyway and prances off alone into the night. She has always been alone, but somehow one gets the feeling that she never feels that way. The children all flock to her and she always has an ample supply of gum and Certs to pass around. One of those children calls Certs "Nancys!"

Children are not the only ones to receive from Nancy's bounty. The adults all know that she will slip them a goodie sometime during the time they are with her. No matter how sad and gloomy you feel, she makes it "all better" when she smilingly hands you a stick of gum.

Each week she places her order at the local grocery for a case of gum and a case of Certs. One week, a different person took her order and thought she meant a box of each instead of a case of each. Needless to say, she was very frustrated when she arrived to pick up her order. She was so worried that there wouldn't be enough to go around! Finally, the woman who usually took her order arrived on the scene and Nancy was happy again.

The next time you hear someone say they can't do anything or that they just don't have any talent, ask them if they have ever passed out gum! Paul explains:

> **Now there are varieties of gifts, but the same Spirit. And there are varieties of ministries, and the same Lord. And there are varieties of effects, but the same God who works all things in all persons. . .But one and the same Spirit works all these things, distributing to each one individually just as He wills. . .For the body is not one member, but many. . .But now God has placed the members, each one of them, in the body, just as He desired.**
>
> **—I Corinthians 12:4-6, 11, 14, 18**
> **New American Standard Bible**

I am glad He placed Nancy in the body. Where did He place you?

This was written in 1984. Nancy has since gone on to be with the Lord. She was a member of Hampton Christian Church in Hampton, Tennessee.

Dog Poop

Okay, okay—I know it's a gross title for a story, but that's what it's about, so that's what I'm calling it! So there!

All of us have done it—stepped in dog poop. Well, today I did it! The thing is, you never discover it until you are in the car. All of a sudden the odor starts wafting upwards toward everyone's noses. Someone says, "Ugh! What is that?"

Someone else says, "Check your shoes."

Next, the person who did it screams, "Pull the car over!"

Usually in our family, it's my husband, who does it. We call him "The Poop Magnet!" Today, I confess, it was me. Tommy, John thomas and I had gotten up at 5:30 this morning to go help Jason paint a house he is fixing up. Most of the time, I was standing on the porch, but somehow as I was walking around the outside, it happened! Instead of trying to clean it up in the car, I just took my shoe off and put it into a plastic bag until we got home. Then I sat it outside beside the water hose and came inside to get a shower. After I got out of the shower, I looked out the bedroom window and saw Tommy cleaning the poop off my shoe! Now, in all the years we have been married, I have never cleaned the poop off his shoe! Why did he do that? Because that's what he does. He cleans up the poop in all of our lives. It doesn't have to be dog poop on a shoe. Whenever any of us steps into a mess, no matter how nasty, Tommy cleans it up. I won't list all the poop that all of us have "stepped" in over the years, but I can tell you that it always got cleaned up. We knew when we messed up that Daddy would fix it! I also can't tell you how safe that makes our boys and me feel. Not only does he clean up the poop in our lives, he also tries to clean it up in others' lives outside the family.

Our Heavenly Father does the same thing. We keep stepping in poop and He keeps cleaning it up. I want to be a person who cleans up poop for other people, don't you? The soap, brush and water hose are waiting. Let's get to work!

The Eclipse

It was a perfect night for it—clear, crisp and very cool, even though it was July. Our adventure started when our family went for our nightly jog. Our favorite place took us by a hundred-year-old covered bridge and along the Doe River. As we approached the bridge, the full moon shone over the bridge and reflected in the water below. It looked like a harvest moon—a beautiful, deep orange. It was breathtakingly beautiful, and I felt God must have painted the scene just for us. As we continued running, we talked about the moon and the eclipse that was to take place about 1:30 the next morning. It was the first total eclipse in a hundred years! We made plans to stay up and watch it. Our oldest son John thomas (the scientist!) informed us that it was to turn red after the eclipse. I commented that the moon turning to blood meant that the Lord could come back that night! As we ran, we discussed how we all felt about that. Our youngest son Jason just listened and took it all in.

As we reached our destination and were running back, he looked at my husband and said,

"You know, Dad, if Jesus does come tonight, I think I'll be ready."

As we sat huddled together on the front porch that night covered with blankets and watching the eclipse, I thought of Jason's comment over and over. No wonder Jesus said we must be converted and become as little children!

8th and Jane St.

One day in late November, Tommy was out of town and John thomas and I were in "the city" at Barnes and Noble Bookstore. He was looking for a CD, so I told him I wanted to look at the Christmas books, and for him to pick me up on his way out. I picked up a couple and flipped through them. Then my eye caught a little book at the back of the table called <u>Christmas on Jane Street</u> by Billy Romp. It is the wonderful true story of a family from Vermont that comes to New York City every year at Christmastime to sell trees in the West Village. I picked it up and started reading it. It was delightful! I didn't buy it then, but went back for it at the first of the week when Tommy came home.

Thanksgiving week, our friends Dean, Amy and Luke Mathis came to visit, and the day after Thanksgiving we all got on the train and went to Greenwich Village and Jane Street. I spotted the lights before anyone else, then the trees and the little camper. I practically ran the rest of the way up 8th Avenue to Jane Street. It was all and more than I had imagined, and standing outside the camper was Billy Romp and his son Henry! I couldn't believe it! I introduced myself and they hugged me. Then Henry ran and got his sister Ellie. Billy's wife Patti was inside the tiny camper nursing their infant, Timmy. After they all signed my book, Henry went to work. He was helping sell this night and he took charge. He picked out a tree he thought I would like, then priced it for me. Forty-five dollars!

"Too high," I said.

"Okay," he said. "How about thirty?"

I've never paid over twenty dollars for a tree, but this year was different. This was the Romps and it was Jane Street in New York City and it was magical! I would have paid fifty had he persisted! Seven-year-old Henry sawed off the bottom of the tree. Finally, I asked Henry to pick me out some branches to decorate with. He gave me extra. Billy drilled a hole in the bottom of the tree, bound it with string and we carried it home on the train.

What a wonderful experience!

What a wonderful family!

I hope this story will help make your Christmas as special and magical as it has made ours. I hope that it will give you a little bit of insight into why we have fallen in love with New York!

The Fern

It was a spindly little thing when she gave it to me, with only about three fronds. But then, she was such a frail little thing herself, looking back it seems appropriate. "See if you can do anything with it," she said. "All of my other plants have died. I just can't care for them as I once did." So saying, she presented me with her three-fronded fern!

My mother was dying of cancer, and though I was putting on a brave front, it was very hard for me to accept the fact that this one upon whom I had depended for so many years was now becoming increasingly dependent upon me. I could remember times when I brought my plants to Mother for her to "revive." It seemed to me there was not anything she could not do.

Thanksgiving of that year, the doctors gave her six months to live. Six months later, in the spring when everything was coming to life again, she died. Deep down, I knew she wasn't dead, but my thoughts were a little clouded and I was too caught up in my grief to emphasize the positive. I mostly wanted to push the whole thing out of my mind. I went back home and got on with the business of "living."

In the meantime, I kept trying to nurse that puny fern, wanting to throw it away, but hesitating because she had asked me to take care of it. Finally, the weather became warm enough so that I could put it outside. All summer it sat on the porch—neglected most of the time—but occasionally I would remember and water it. Even with the neglect, I noticed through the summer that it seemed to be growing just a little bit. Before long, October came and with it the cold and frost, so the little fern had to come inside. It did all right for a while, but soon parts began turning brown and dropping off. It barely made it through the winter, and I took it back outside in the spring. Again it perked up and grew even larger. As the autumn approached this year, I started to worry. Keeping this little fern alive had suddenly become very important to me. I finally decided to take it to Benny, my florist friend, and see if he had any suggestions.

"The plant is just root bound," he said. "All it needs is a bigger pot."

"Great," I said. "Fix it for me!"

A friend of mine was over the other day and she said, "Your fern is so beautiful and healthy. How do you keep it from turning brown and dying in the winter? Mine do terribly when I bring them inside."

"Just put it in a bigger pot," I said. Then it hit me! My mother could not go on living here—it was too confining. She needed a larger space if she were to continue growing. My mother's fern is 36 inches across and 26 inches high. In fact, it is filling up this pot! My mother is growing in ways I can't even imagine. But unlike the fern, her capacity for growth is not restricted to a pot! For a Christian, death is only a doorway into a broader existence—a replanting, but not in a limited container. There are no limitations in Heaven and no danger of becoming "root-bound."

I still miss my mother, and I cannot wait to see how she has "grown." I only hope she can see growth in me.

The Fifteenth Floor

We were staying in a second-floor room in a hotel high up in the Smoky Mountains. It was a good floor to be on. It didn't take very long for the elevator to get there, and we had a full view of the lobby below from the balcony that ran all the way around on each floor. We were only there for one weekend, and we had picked a place with a pool so that Caleb could swim. Our seventeen-month old grand daughter, Gillian, wasn't quite as thrilled with the idea of swimming. She didn't like elevators either, so it was good that we were only on the second floor. Caleb, on the other hand, would not be satisfied until I agreed to ride to the fifteenth floor with him. I really didn't want to. I liked the second floor. It felt safe to me. We had a good view of the mountains. From the inside balcony, we could see the people in the lobby below, and strings of light stretching above us to the fifteenth floor. I was content on the second floor.

Caleb calls me Prisha, and all weekend, he begged, "Prisha, please! Let's go to the fifteenth floor!"

"Okay," I said. "We will. . .sometime."

His Daddy rode to the fifteenth floor with him, as did his Mommy, and my husband (Papa). Each time, Caleb came back with glowing reports. "You won't believe it, Prisha!" he would say. To tell the truth, I was a little scared of such a great height, and thought that it surely couldn't look much different from the second floor. Finally, just before we checked out of the hotel, I agreed to ride with Caleb to the fifteenth floor. We entered the elevator and I stood next to the solid door. As we ascended, I moved timidly to the glass front of the car and peeked out. When we got to the fifteenth floor, I said, "That was fun Caleb. Let's go back now." I started to punch the button for the second floor when he said what I had feared he would say all along: "Oh, no, Prisha! We have to get out of the elevator and look down. You won't believe it!" So, of course, I did.

It was spectacular! It was breathtaking! It was beyond imagination! Suddenly, I knew I would never be content with the second floor again. After a few minutes, we reluctantly stepped onto the elevator for the descent. On the way down, Caleb said, "You know what, Prisha? I wish we lived here so that I could go to the fifteenth floor every day!" So do I, Caleb. Quite frankly, my life will never be the same because I have had a taste of what it is like to view the world from the fifteenth floor. Thank you, Caleb. I love you.

ON THE WAY BACK UP

Copyright © 2003, Solbong Kim & John thomas Oaks
Caliora Music Publishing, ASCAP

It's a painful trip that leads you to the bottom

And I guess ev'rybody takes it now and then

Some would see it as a final destination

But it's as good a place as any to begin

So when you're face-down on the pavement

And you feel that no one cares

Don't sit there staring up the steps

You could be stepping up the stairs

On the way back up you find your balance
There's a hand to hold within your reach
If you listen close enough
You can hear a voice that's teach-
ing you the answer
On the way back up

On the way back up you look for answers
And along the way you find some friends
And the higher that you climb
You find your sanity depends
On who you lean on
On the way back up

Who you lean on
Who you trust
Can look like gold and turn to dust
And people blow away like whispers on a wind
There's only one who you can lean on till the end

On the way back up the view is brighter

Ev'ry step you take the burdens lift

When you turn a new direction

You can feel the outcome shift

To your advantage

On the way back up

From the April, 2003 Juilliard Premiere
of the one-act musical, "On The Way Down"
Music by Solbong Kim
Lyrics by John thomas Oaks
Book by Tommy Oaks

The Gold Combs

I noticed her coming through the front door of the store as I was making my way up the aisle to leave. I could tell it was a struggle for her to open the door, but I was too far away to see why. As I got closer, I understood. Her slight body was bent and twisted almost as if someone had placed her the way they wanted her years ago and bound her until she stopped growing. She could hardly walk, but she did walk—with a sort of sliding motion, her feet bent to the inside. She had crutches—the kind that form a bracelet around the lower part of the arm. I stood and watched her shuffle and slide as she made her way down an aisle to the right of the door. But it wasn't her crippled body that held me so spellbound. It was her. Her face was perfectly made up—rouge, eyeliner, lipstick—the works. She was dressed impeccably—a splash of color around her neck in the form of a scarf. And then I saw them—poised majestically on the back of her head were two gold combs. They were not small, unobtrusive combs, but large, ornate, glittering combs—combs that caught the light and the attention of anyone looking her way. I stood transfixed by them. She was walking toward the accessories section of the store (scarves, gloves, etc.). No longer did she seem to be shuffling and dragging. Those combs had transformed her into an elegant lady dressed for the dance, gliding across a ballroom floor—perhaps Cinderella on the way to meet her Prince Charming? Maybe that's how she intended it to be. Maybe she wanted everyone's attention diverted from her crippled body to the gold combs. Maybe she was saying, "Don't look at my body, look at my soul. Inside, I am beautiful. Inside, I shine. Inside, I glitter. And I wore these gold combs just to let you know."

Googie

Gillian's nickname is "Googie." One day when she was five years old, Googie and I were sitting in the swing on the porch. I was reading to her. There was a drawing of a grandmother in the story. Googie said, "Grandmothers are OLD!"

I said, "Really? Well—I'm your grandmother, Googie. Do you think I'm old?"

She thought for a minute, and then she said, "No. You're NEW!"

I love that! Here's to all the grandmothers who are NEW!!

I love you, Googie!

By the way—
my grandchildren call me, "Prisha."
I love that, too!

The Greatest Show on Earth

I took my boys to the circus last night. I thought surely it would not be as good as it was when I was small, and I was right—it was better! Granted, the smell of sawdust and musty tent was not there, for it was held indoors. But it was far more glamorous and sophisticated. It was also more dangerous. No nets were used! Some used guide wires, but not all. A few plunged right into their performance heedless of the danger involved.

I came home as excited as the boys. We kept interrupting each other in our haste to describe it all to Daddy, who could not go. The circus had come to town! Each act had practiced until they were confident and could perform with finesse and style. The music was beautiful and played with precision and perfection. One could tell long hours of practice and hard work had gone into the preparation for the performance. The ringmaster spoke with eloquence and command. He was precise and to the point. He held our attention, and sometimes we were all very quiet and in awe. But there were other times when we laughed till the tears rolled. The music, the speaker, the majesty and beauty had us coming away from the circus full of sheer joy at the wonder of it all.

Tomorrow we are going to church. . .

Grow Lovely Growing Old

It snowed last night. Tonight, I'm sitting in front of the fire just enjoying being cozy. My two boys are playing and talking. I'm eavesdropping. John thomas said something about when he gets to be thirty-two, and Jason said that would be OLD! Naturally at this point I had to put my two cents worth in: "Do you think Mommy is old?"

Jason answered, "No."

Then I said, "Do you think I'm young?"

Again he answered, "No."

I said, "Well, what AM I?"

He said, "You're just Mommy!"

I guess mommies and daddies are ageless and timeless. I wish that were true, but since it isn't, I hope I can fill my days with love and beauty for my children and everyone I meet. You and I have both known people whose age would indicate that they were old, but their steps were lively, their minds were keen and alive and there was a sparkle and warmth in their eyes that made it seem as if life were just beginning for them. I want to be like that. Assuming you might want this sparkle too, how can you and I accomplish this? Having observed the older generation for quite some time (and not far from being part of it myself), I have a few very simple suggestions to make to help us stay young.

1. Don't sit down when you need to move.

2. Don't dwell too much on the past (especially the same stories!).

3. Tell people what you are going to be when you grow up, and mean it! Have some goals for the future.

4. Be constantly and consistently doing things for other people.

5. Visit old people. Remember—you aren't old!

6. Stay around children and young people a lot. Observe how simple things make children happy.

7. Walk every day—out of doors. If that isn't possible, touch your toes and do deep knee bends. I talked to an eighty-year-old woman who said she touches her toes

twenty-five times each morning and walks a mile and a half every day to get a newspaper. Do you wonder why she doesn't let the newspaper boy deliver it? I don't!

8. Don't tell everyone you meet how bad you feel. Tell them you feel great, and you will probably begin to believe it yourself before long!

9. Above all, don't feel sorry for yourself. Life is meant to be lived—not endured.

You may have already thought of all these things. My next suggestion is—do them! I am not saying that all of your problems, worries, sadness and heartache will leave and never come back. I am not even saying that you should never tell anyone your problems or seek advice from a friend. I am saying that if you do these things, the problems may not seem quite so important and maybe, just maybe, you'll be happier.

Let me grow lovely growing old—
So many fine things to do;
Laces and ivory and gold,
And silks need not be new;
And there is healing in old trees
Old streets a glamour hold;
Why may not I, as well as these
Grow lovely, growing old?

—Arval B. Burton

From one hopeful lovely to another—
Here's to tomorrow. . .

and tomorrow. . .

and

t   o   m   o   r   r   o   w. . .

A Halloween Father's Day Story

It was a windy, eerie Halloween night, and the wind was the type that makes old-timers and children of old-timers say, "It's blowin' up somethin' out there!" It seemed to blow in with the sole purpose of adding spookiness to the night. As the evening progressed, there was a feeling in the air of impending doom, but I attributed it to the holiday. I was talking on the phone when it happened.

My son and the little girl next door came running in with horrified expressions on their faces. Someone had slit our puppy Tiffany's leg from top to bottom! I ran outside. The cut was huge and deep, but not bleeding very much. Tiffany was crying and so were the children. I was about to, also!

But this story is not about Halloween or the tragedy of our puppy, but about the great love of a daddy for his children and their beloved pet.

The boys' daddy very tenderly picked up Tiffany and put
her in the truck and drove to the vet twenty-five miles
away. About midnight, he returned carrying a sleepy puppy
full of stitches. She also had a huge bandage on her leg.
My husband did not go to bed. "Our" daddy got a hammer
and nails, two pieces of lumber and a tarpaulin and
constructed a lean-to on the front porch. Under it, he made
a soft bed for Tiffany. The wind was blowing so hard he
had to nail the tarp to the front porch. Then, very carefully,
he carried Tiffy to her bed and placed a bowl of water at
her head. Only then did we go to bed.

After we were in bed, I thought to myself, *How many
daddies would have done that?* Some would have left her
in the yard and said, "It's only a dog." Many years after
this incident, she literally saved Jason, our youngest son,
from being bitten by a copperhead by jumping on it and
taking three bites to her leg. We thought she would lose the
leg, but the Lord saw fit to heal her completely!

In a world of uncaring, too-busy daddies, it's a joy to find a daddy who goes the extra mile. It's a joy to have a daddy who makes every day a happy, special day for his two boys and wife.

Happy February!

This was written over thirty years ago!

There are so many ways to say, "I love you." My little five-year-old came up to me the other day and said, "Mommy, you're the cutest thing!" My nine-year-old hugged me the other night and said, "You're the best Mommy in the whole world." I had to go upstairs for a few minutes after supper one night, and when I came back down, my thirty-year-old husband had cleared the supper dishes off the table!

There are so many ways to say, "I love you." Find one today. And if all else fails—just say it!

Have You Stopped?

I had to go my son's ball game an hour early one night. He had to have his picture taken, and I knew I would have an hour to sit in the bleachers. I took my cross stitch to work on. Another game was going on, but I was oblivious to it since my son was not yet on the court. A little four-year-old girl was not particularly interested either. She kept walking up and down the bleachers. Each time she went down, she put her hand on my back to balance herself. Somewhere in the process of her ascent and descent, she paused and watched me for a while. "What are you doing?" she asked.

"This is called cross stitch," I answered. "Does your mother know how to do this?"

"Oh, yes!" she said. "My mother can do everything!"

There is a time in all of our lives when we believe that our mothers can do everything. . .somewhere along the line, we stop thinking that.

There is a time in all of our lives when we believe that our heavenly Father can do everything. . .

I Believe in. . .

One night just before Christmas, Papa, Googie and I were on our way to the grocery store. From the back seat a little voice said, "Prisha, ask me if I believe in Santa Claus." "Googie, do you believe in Santa Claus?" I asked. Again, from the back seat, "No, silly—I believe in cashmere from Burlington Coat Factory!" (Obviously a commercial she had heard, but coming from a six year old, pretty funny.)

I've told that story a lot because I thought it was so cute. Then I started thinking about it in a slightly different manner. When some people are faced with that question concerning Jesus, their answer is just as ridiculous. It isn't funny and cute like Googie's answer—It's sad and tragic.

Do you believe in Jesus?
No, silly—I believe in Buddha.
I believe in Mohammed.
I believe in myself.

I believe in money.

I believe in America.

I believe in fate.

I believe in hard work.

I believe in a good job.

I believe in fame.

I believe in knowing the right people.

I believe in world peace.

I believe in negotiating.

I believe in survival of the fittest.

I believe in saving the environment.

Do you believe in Jesus?

No, silly—I believe in cashmere from Burlington Coat Factory!

Jeannie

Jeannie does have "light brown hair," and beautiful, large brown eyes and extremely long eyelashes. Many people would tell you that Jeannie is lucky to have the parents she has, but I think her parents are the lucky ones. So do her parents.

I do not know what Jeannie thinks about the matter. Jeannie cannot talk. Furthermore, Jeannie cannot walk. She can't sit, either. She cannot feed herself, and often

even has trouble swallowing. But she can laugh—Oh, can
she ever laugh! It isn't a tiny giggle—it's an infectious,
deep hilarious laugh. She makes me laugh,
too—and everyone in the room with her. Many times my
husband has had to stop his sermon so that all of us could
have a good laugh with Jeannie. She thinks his sermons are
hilarious!

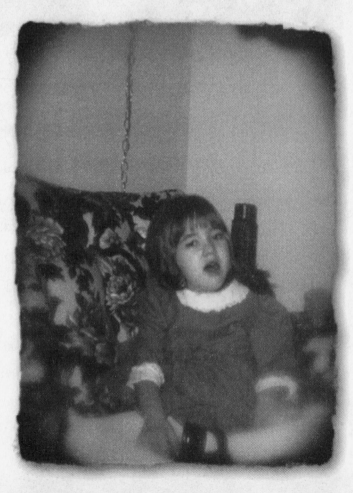

Jeannie is a very beautiful ten-year-old who never speaks to you when you go to visit. She never tells you she loves you. She never says, "Goodbye, and please come again soon. I've enjoyed our visit." But every inch of her says, "I'm so glad you're here. I love you so much. Please, can't you stay longer?" She has "spoken" more to me in the years I have known her than some of the greatest orators of our time. She has shown more love than some church members with whom I have been associated for thirty years. And yet, there were those who said she would be better off in a home. A home? She is in the happiest of homes with her mother, daddy and little sister.

There was one doctor who said that some surgery her parents inquired about would not help, and besides, they only liked to help those whom they felt could be useful to society. Useful to society? Jeannie is not only useful to society—she is necessary! She has affected my life in ways that no other human being ever has. I have seen people's lives change drastically for the good as a direct result of her influence.

There are those who would tell you she is handicapped. Handicapped? I say we are the ones who are handicapped. We are the ones with all the hang-ups and inhibitions and hate and jealousy and greed. Jeannie is the perfect one.

But Jeannie can't talk.

Teresa Jeanine Morton
September 13, 1968 - February 22, 1986

Job and His Friends

An old saying goes:

> **A friend in need**
> **Is a friend indeed**

Job was certainly a man in need and he did have friends. His friends, however, remind me of the type of people my husband has often spoken of who teach us how not to act. Since we all have times when our friends are in need, it is good to reflect on how Job's friends treated him.

In a book by Eugenia Price, <u>No Pat Answers</u>, she refers repeatedly to the clichés and phrases that people often use when trying to comfort someone. One thesis of her book is that there are times when no answer is better than a pat one. When my friends' child died, their grief was made greater at times by some of the comments that were made by friends.

Job's friends sat in silence with him for seven days and seven nights.

—Job 2:13

Perhaps this is all anyone really wants in a time like this. Maybe just your presence says more than any comment you could ever make.

Blessed be the God and Father of our Lord Jesus Christ, the Father of mercies and God of all comfort, who comforts us in all our tribulation, that we may be able to comfort those who are in any trouble, with the comfort with which we ourselves are comforted by God.

—2 Corinthians 1:3,4

Eliphaz (one of Job's friends) makes the comment, "If I say something, will you get mad at me? Well, even if you do, I just have to say it." *(Job 4:1,2—my translation)* To say, "I'm saying this for your own good," can be questionable. Sometimes I think we just want to sound pious. Job might not have complained to God *(7:20; 10:2; 30:20)* if his friends had just remained quiet and not hinted that the reason for Job's suffering was his sin *(4:7; 8:6; 22:5).*

The first congregation my husband and I ministered with was in Meadowview, Virginia. A member of that church was a wonderful woman and good friend named Hester. Whenever anyone had a death in the family or any kind of trouble, Hester never called to say, "Let me know if I can do anything." She just went to their home and started doing! I'm sure with all the trouble Job was having, he could have used some financial and physical help. His friends could have helped clean up the mess from the tornado *(1:19)*. No doubt there were funeral arrangements and cooking and cleaning for relatives to take care of. If the friends' wives had pitched in and helped Job's wife with all she had to do, maybe she would not have lashed out at Job *(2:9)*. Job was probably in need of some money, too, since all his worldly possessions had been taken away *(1:14-17)*. Since he was taken ill *(2:7)*, he probably didn't get workman's comp or disability, so he missed all those days at whatever work he did. Job's friends were obviously financially independent enough that they were able to take all those days off from work to be with Job. They could have given him money, but there's no record that they even offered to.

When the days of questions were over, most of the friends' comments seemed negative and rebuking:

Eliphaz said, "Who ever perished being innocent?" *(4:7)*

Bildad said, "If you were pure and upright, surely now He would awake for you." *(8:6)*

Zophar said, "Should no one rebuke you?" *(11:3)*

If we find ourselves in the situation Job's friends were in and decide to offer some choice "words of wisdom," let's determine that they will be positive words.

> **Let no corrupt communication proceed out of your mouth, but what is good for necessary edification, that it may impart grace to the hearers.**
>
> —Ephesians 4:29

Matthew 5:4 says, "Blessed are those who mourn, for they shall be comforted." I want to be one of those who comforts by being helpful and especially by being quiet—unless I have something positive to say.

Just Listen

Why do many of us feel it is our duty to give advice—whether it is asked for or not? Don't we have enough to do keeping our own lives straight? I am sure my sister gets tired of my unending advice. Has it ever occurred to any of us that perhaps someone just wants a friend to listen? Our advice may be great for us, but often I feel my advice is resented—and well it should be. The person I am offering advice to may have been going to do the very thing I offered advice about, but because he felt I was being pushy and trying to run his life, he may do just the opposite out of spite. I can't really blame anyone for doing that. I have felt that way myself. Especially if someone says to me, "If you do so-and-so, you are making the biggest mistake of your life."

My reaction is, "Well, I'll just prove you wrong!"

Occasionally a friend will ask advice. When this happens, I try to prayerfully consider any remarks I could make and then make as few as possible. I would like to be able to steer the person in a direction to help him work out his problem himself rather than giving him a step-by-step diagram to follow. Parents have an especially hard time with this, even after a child is grown and on his own!

"Your hair is too long. You need to go to the barber shop."

"Your hair is too short. You need to let it grow!"

"I don't care what kind of clothes you like. It's my money, and I'm not spending it on wild-looking clothes." *Note: They are probably no wilder than the clothes you liked as a teenager!*

"You should go to college here."

"You should get a degree in this. You'll make more money."

"You shouldn't buy that. You should save your money for this."

"Well, if you want MY opinion. . ."

I usually want to scream, "I DON'T!!!" Most of the time, if people want your advice, they will ask. Until then, just listen.

Kindest Act
The Story of a High School Boy

When our son was six years old, he took swimming lessons
at the high school. The last night, parents were invited for
a closing program in which the children would perform the
strokes they had learned and attempt something they had
never tried before—a jump from the diving board. Each
child took a turn. Some were very brave, running out and
jumping in. Others were somewhat hesitant, tiptoeing out
and giving it some thought before leaping. Finally, it was
our son's turn. He looked very apprehensive as he crept out
to the edge. He peered down at the water, then backed
away. He crept forward again, but again he hesitated. One
of the high school boys who had been one of the instructors
saw him and walked over. "Come on," he said gently.
"You can do it. I'll stand right here close."

My little boy tried again and again. Finally, he turned and
walked off the board. It was very quiet, so everyone heard

the voice that hissed, "Chicken!"

That did it. Our son turned and ran to where we were sitting, crying all the way. The high school boy followed him and said to him very softly, "Hey, John thomas—want to try again? I'll stay as long as you want me to. You don't have to jump until you're ready." John thomas wiped his eyes, grinned and walked back to the board.

In the meantime, the other children had finished the exhibition and the parents were getting up to leave. When our little boy walked back to the diving board, however, they all stopped. A hush fell over the crowd. John thomas walked to the edge, looked down, looked to his encourager and jumped! I cried this time as a cheer went up from the crowd.

I want to pay tribute to those young people who are kind and who care—especially our son's hero.

The Lesson

I had been called to substitute teach for a second grade class. One little girl was obviously not as financially "well-off" as some of the other children in the class. Her clothes were not quite as current. She was not as clean as she could have been, but what drew me to her was her head. She had a bald spot from the front to the back of her head about the width of an electric razor. A scar ran all the way down this bald spot.

At recess, even though the air was chilly, I needed to get out into the fresh air as much as I felt the children needed it, so out we went. I stood under a tree wrapped in my coat and watched to be sure no one was doing anything to get hurt. The little girl stood close to me.

I asked her about herself—her name, her age, her family—and then I asked her about the scar. She said she had to have an operation, and that her cousin had had the same one. She said they had to have steel plates put inside their heads. We stood together for a while watching the other children play.

After a couple of minutes two other little girls with long, shiny hair and dressed in the latest little girl fashions came running up. As children tend to do, they started running around and around me, using me as the shield to keep one from catching the other. I asked them what they were playing. "House," they said. "One is the Mommie and the other her little girl. She won't come in for supper."

"Can I play?" my little friend asked. There was no response. Suddenly the two little girls broke away and started running across the school yard, the wind tossing their hair. The memory of their prettiness and the wind in their hair will always be with me.

"Can I play?" she called again after them. Then came one of those wonderful, bittersweet moments that happens quickly and is gone, but that makes all of life make sense. One of the little girls turned and called back, "Yes, you can play with us."

As the child of poverty chased after the children of plenty, they seemed to merge as one—just three little girls having a wonderful time, racing with the wind, playing and laughing and enjoying life.

I thought, "That's as it should be—all of us playing and laughing, happy and carefree, not looking at what the other has on or which of us is ugly or pretty, scarred or unscarred—just enjoying each other and living together in harmony."

The Lilac Tree

We had a freeze warning last night, but I don't see anything
that has been hurt. My jonquils seem to have made it just
fine, but I can't tell about my lilac tree yet.

Every time I see a lilac tree, I go back fifty years to a small,
yellow house on a tree-lined street where I grew up. Just
outside our kitchen door was a huge lilac tree—at least it
was big to me. I can remember the hummingbirds drinking
from it. It was my mother's favorite flower, and every
spring she brought bunches into the house. I can still see
her bustling around the kitchen fixing peanut butter and
oatmeal cookies (those were better for us!). I can still smell
the mingled odor of baking cookies and lilacs. Our cookie
jar was always full, and so were our lives. Late in the
evening, Mama would sit out in the yard with us and we
would catch lightning bugs in a jar with holes punched in
the lid. The odor of the lilacs seemed to get stronger as
night came on. Before we went in for the night, we always
released our little "lanterns" so they wouldn't die.

It was under this same tree that my little sister sat her turtle one day so he could get a suntan! She picked a spot where the sun filtered between the lilac blooms and left him there. We learned that day that tiny turtles can't take strong sunlight. We both cried. She only planned to leave him there a little while, but. . .well. . .you can guess the rest.

Oh, the memories that can come from just one thing, like a tree in our yard! I also recall another tree that creates memories—the tree our Lord was crucified on that bleak Friday so long ago. Those memories are not so happy. He hung there and died there so that we could have happy memories now, and look forward to happiness for all eternity.

At the end of your life, will you have happy memories, or only recollections of turtles left too long in the sun?

Love Letters in the Cookie Jar

Have you ever found a love letter in the cookie jar? How about in the lunch box—on the mirror—under your pillow—pinned to a shirt packed in your suitcase— scribbled in the middle of a sermon left lying on the desk or on the windshield of your car? In our family, love letters are left everywhere. About four years ago, my husband tore out a tiny heart about the size of a half dollar and wrote, "I love you," on it. I still have it (along with many others he has written!). Our boys leave love notes all over the place, from the cookbook to the bathroom mirror.

I remember a particularly discouraging day when I did not even love myself. How, then, could I expect anyone else to love me? It was late and I had tucked the boys in for the night. I dragged myself into my bedroom and reached to pull the cover down on the bed. Something caught my eye on the quilt at the foot of the bed. Jason had left a pile of

his play money lying there. As I reached to pick it up, I
noticed a note beside it. Written in Jason's childlike scrawl,
it said, "Mom, your (sic) worth a lot more than this. I love
you, Jason."

Another time I walked into the bathroom to find a big heart
drawn on the mirror with, "I love you," written in the
middle. John thomas was the culprit this time. I had to buy
new lipstick, but I didn't mind! For about a month it was
hard to see in our bathroom mirror. None of us could bring
ourselves to wipe it off!

All of us need to hear, "I love you," and we need to read it,
too. John Greenall says:

> **A telephone call from a friend is a joy, unless you are
> in the middle of a meal, having a bath, or on the point
> of going out to an engagement for which you are
> already late. But even when you have time, a
> telephone conversation cannot be savored and rerun
> several times as a letter can. You cannot put a blue**

ribbon around a sentimental telephone call and keep it for years. A letter sender in effect is saying, "I am setting aside some of my time for you alone. I am thinking of you. This is more important to me than all the other things I could be doing."

Someone you know may need a love note. Tape it to his or her front door. Put it in one of their shoes. Write it on a balloon. Send it through the mail. Tape it to the refrigerator. However you do it, do it today—right now! People need to know they are loved.

Think I'll go and have a cookie. . .

The Luggage and the Ring

Our oldest son, John thomas, was asked to come to a church in Indiana to help with worship for about three months. About halfway through his stay, he had to come home for a previous engagement. On the way back, the airline lost his luggage. No big deal. It happens all the time. They just bring it out when the next flight comes in. This time, they couldn't find it! He flew in on Monday. Tuesday—no luggage. Wednesday—no luggage. Rehearsal for the worship band was on Thursday and all his charts were in that suitcase! He called late Wednesday night and said, "Mom, pray!" After I hung up, I started praying even harder than I had been. I told the Lord, "You know exactly where that luggage is. Please get it to him."

John thomas was staying in Duane and Joyce Sword's storage barn that had been converted into an apartment. It was located in an Indiana cornfield on State Route

Something-or-Other in the middle of nowhere! Ten minutes
after I hung up, the phone rang again. I was still praying.
It was John thomas. He said, "As soon as I got off the
phone with you, my cell phone rang and a guy said, 'I think
I have your luggage, but I can't find your house.'
So I looked out the window and saw headlights driving
slowly by about 150 yards away at the end of the driveway.
I walked out on the porch, turned on the light and waved
my arms. 'Is that you on the porch?' the guy asked.
I said, 'Yep!'
So he pulled in the driveway and dropped my bags off!"

I told my friend Kim this story. She had recently joined
Tommy's CD-of-the-month club *(which you can also do if
you go to* tommyoaks.com *and sign up!)*. Jokingly, he told
her that she would receive a secret decoder ring for joining.
About a month later, I got an indignant email from Kim
wanting to know where her ring was. A few days later, I
was in Party City and since it was February, they had their
Valentine stuff out. I was just browsing, when my eye fell
upon a ring with a huge "ruby" in it that glowed when the

gem was twisted. They also had a heart-shaped velvet box on the shelf, so I bought both and put them in the mail with instructions on how to use the ring. Later that week, I received another email complaining that the ring was defective! I wrote back, "Did you twist the stone to the left?" Yes, she had twisted the stone to the left, and the secret decoder ring was still defective. A few days later, another email arrived from Kim which I will share with you almost word-for-word. John thomas was on his way to her church that Friday night to do a comedy show with his friend John Branyan, and Kim was trying to arrange her schedule so she could go.

Dearest poaks,

You will not believe how dense I can be! Just a few minutes ago, I was lying in bed wondering how in the world I ever got in the "mess" I'm in. I'm lying there thinking about the story of Jt's luggage and thinking how nothing like that ever happens to me. The stories I tell end after the praying. Nothing happens—the end. Basically, I'm lying in bed thinking such pitiful thoughts (pitiful, but truthful). The past ten days have been horrible. I've missed sleep, I've missed

work, I haven't seen my friends (and on and on I whine). I'm lying there feeling lonely, overwhelmed and very very tired and sad, and I look over by my lamp and see this heart-shaped box. I open the box, put on this fancy ring that was inside and turn the whole ring around. Now pay attention—I turn the whole ring around my finger begging God if I can please have Friday night, when lo and behold, I see the gem on the ring appears to be a little loose. . .so I turn it. DUH! It glows!! Am I a candidate for the idiot of the year award?!?! Another laugh and cry. I tried to stay in bed, but it was tooo funny! So I got up, turned the computer on and wrote this email. I have such a sorry life. Hi-lite of my month is a ring that glows! I'm off to bed and I shall sleep with it, and with it glowing (I hope the light won't burn out! But I don't care!). I needed a comfort to sleep tonight, and who would have thunk it to be a plastic red glow-in-the-dark magic secret decoder ring?

Here is my answer back to her:

Dear Kim,
All I can say is, "Well, DUH—" Why do you think I kept telling

you to turn the stone to the left? What a wonderful story—
and just like the Lord! You really didn't need the stone to
glow until last night. It glowed when it was supposed to!
That story made me so excited, I just started laughing out
loud—and I'm here by myself! As for Friday night, I believe
the Lord wants you to go. Someone else may not, so
perhaps you will have to do a little extra planning.
Don't give up. There is an answer. Just because you don't
know what it is doesn't mean there isn't one. You might have
to look for them, but there are answers. I am praying. The
luggage will come when you lest expect it. The ring will glow
when you least expect it. I love you and will steep up the
prayers for Friday night.

Luggage arrives, rings glow, and guess what? Kim got to
go to the show!

Thank you, Duane and Joyce
for your friendship and hospitality!

The Manger Rearranger

My husband and I had been living in New York City with our oldest son and had come home to Tennessee for the Christmas holidays. I could hardly wait to get all the decorations out and put the Christmas music on.

I especially looked forward to putting the manger scene in its place of honor. We have had the manger scene for over thirty years. Our boys have grown up with it and always enjoyed unpacking it and setting it up as much as I did. This year, I set it up. I very carefully and symmetrically arranged the shepherds, wise men and animals around the outside of the stable gazing in on Mary, Joseph and baby Jesus.

Our grandbaby Caleb who had just turned five came to visit with our younger son Jason and daughter-in-law Misty. He was fascinated by the manger scene and played with it while he was there. There is a music box on the side of the stable that plays "Silent Night," and he would wind it up and play with the figures while it played.

My son's family stayed for a couple of days. The night they left, I was tidying up the house. On my way through the living room, I eventually reached the manger scene. My carefully placed "just-so" figures were all bunched and crowded into a tight little group, blocking the entrance into the stable. All the animals were collected inside around the base of the manger. My orderly instinct kicked in, and I quickly rearranged my manger scene back to its original, tidy presentation. Stepping back to look at my handiwork, I was satisfied that it had been returned to its proper state.

As I turned to walk away, I stopped. What was I thinking? Caleb had the right idea. Instead of keeping our safe little distance from Jesus, we should be crowded together trying our best to get as close to Him as we can. I wondered, "Why am I content to stand outside the doors of the stable where I can only get a glimpse every now and then? Why am I not trying to place myself in a position where I can gaze at Him continually? Jesus was so right when He said that a little child would lead us.

Thank you, Caleb, for teaching me a great truth this Christmas, 2000. I want you to know that I walked back and placed the figures where you put them. I hope that in the Christmases to come, you will rearrange our manger scene again and again. Thank you, Lord, for sending Your Son, and for sending Caleb into our lives!

Memories

Backward, turn backward,

O time, in your flight,

Make me a child again,

Just for tonight!

—Allen

There are days when I wish I could go back—just for a while. I would like to take my mother's hand again and walk out the road to see the goats at our neighbor's goat farm. It was usually in the evening after supper when we went. I can still remember how soft her hand was.

I would like to take my Daddy's hand and walk to the park on Sunday afternoon, or go to the train depot and watch the trains come in. I can still remember how big his hand was. Why, I didn't think there was anything those hands couldn't do!

I would like once more to have Mother push me in my

swing and say, "How Do you Like To Go Up in a Swing?"
I would like to hear my Daddy call to me in my tree house,
"Now don't you fall, baby!" He'll probably always call me
his baby!

I'd like to have my big brother put me on his shoulders one
more time and take me to get an ice cream, even though all
his buddies didn't take their little sisters along!

I would like to hear my big sister say to me as she snuggled
up to me on Christmas Eve, "If you listen, you can hear the
sleigh bells on the roof!" You know, I think I did a couple
of times!

I'd like—just one more time—to hold my red-haired baby
sister in my lap while I sit in my little red rocker. I would
rock her while Mother got her bath water ready. But after a
while, I would like to come back and give my own family
memories to build dreams on. Here's to happy childhood
memories, and happier still, the memories we are building
now for tomorrow.

Memories of Daddy

I have written about my Mother many times, but today I want to pay tribute to a wonderful daddy, too. My daddy was really too lenient with us. He never spanked us, so now I am grateful that Mother did discipline us.

He grew up in Virginia, the oldest of ten children, and had a lot of responsibility at an early age. He left home at thirteen to go to work on the railroad in Harlan, Kentucky. I often wondered why he seemed to love being with us so much. One would think that with all those brothers and sisters, he would be sick of children, but everything he did was for us. He worked long, hard hours, but still had time for us. He made many of our toys from scraps he got at the junkyard. He made our sleds, scooters and tricycles from scraps. Our backyard had a seesaw and a sliding board, both made from things he found at the junkyard. We also had a swing and a tree house. Daddy thought swings were important, so we had one in the backyard and one in the front yard. Daddy worked the night shift, so every day he would push me in the front yard swing while he waited for his ride.

Sunday afternoons, he would take us to the park to play, or to the train station to watch the trains come in and go out. Then he would come home and take a nap on the couch until church time. That was when my sister and I braided his hair in tiny braids all over his head and tied ribbons on the ends of the braids! He would always get up, look in the mirror, and act surprised at what he saw. We always giggled and giggled, thinking we had "pulled one over" on him!

The best thing about Daddy was that I never felt I was a nuisance. The thing that made me realize this was remembering how Daddy always slept during the day. I didn't think much about it at the time, but when I reflect back on those years, I feel so blessed. We were never told to be quiet because we might wake Daddy—and we could be pretty rowdy! Sometimes we even played right under his bedroom window! I asked him about it years later and he said we never bothered him. Often, Mother would take us on the bus to go shopping and she would always say, "Your Daddy will be up when we get home. It'll be too quiet for him to sleep," and he always was!

I thank God for a Daddy who played with me and loved me and took care of me and who never, never made me feel like I was in the way.

Merry Christmas!

It was "beginning to look a lot like Christmas!" No matter
that this was the year that everyone seemed so concerned
that we say, "Happy holiday!" instead. With all the lights
and tinsel and (wonder of wonders) manger scenes, it sure
looked a lot like Christmas to me!

I had gone to the grocery store and was in one of those self-
checkout lanes. The woman across from me was having
some problems with the computer (imagine that!). She had
a baby in a baby seat. The baby was crying. She also had a
little boy who looked about three years old. As the mother
tried to communicate with the clerk in charge of the
computer, the baby kept screaming louder and louder and
the little boy was dancing from one foot to the other saying
to the clerk over and over, "Merry Christmas! Merry
Christmas! Merry Christmas!" There was on the little face
such purity and wonder and excitement, one got the feeling
that he truly had captured the meaning of the words,
"Merry Christmas!" Finally, his mother hissed, "Be quiet,
Christian! You're bothering this man!" He stood there

defeated for a moment, and then, unable to contain himself and unable to keep the words inside a minute longer, he started it again: "Merry Christmas! Merry Christmas! Merry Christmas!"

The first thing I thought was that Christian was aptly named. This little boy truly was a follower of Christ. He was also setting an example for the rest of us. We are so afraid of what The World" will think that when The World hisses, "Be quiet, Christian!" we are!

After wishing Christian a merry Christmas, I walked out of the store more full of joy than when I had walked in. I wanted to shout at everyone I met, "Merry Christmas! Merry Christmas! Merry Christmas!" Of course, I didn't— but I should have! Perhaps I should start practicing now in February so that next December people around me won't be so shocked when I walk down the street or stand in line at the grocery store and greet everyone with—

Merry Christmas!

Merry Christmas!

Merry Christmas!

Merry Christmas!

—Pat

Mr. Hale's Lesson

I grew up in a small community outside of Knoxville, Tennessee, called Fountain City. It was named after the fountain in the middle of the heart-shaped, manmade lake in the center of town. About two blocks from my house was a small country store. In the summer, I would dance to the store, hopping from the pavement to the grass to keep my feet from burning too badly. I loved going to that store. It had wooden floors that had a very distinct smell. Anyone who grew up going to a school with wooden floors or shopping at a store that had them knows what I mean. In the store were jars filled with candy and bins filled with fresh fruit and vegetables. The meat department at the back had a large butcher block and an electric slicer. Mr. Hale was the owner, and he always wore a big white apron. He was not a very big man, so the apron seemed to cover most of his body! He always sliced the meat and cheese, and his two daughters ran the cash register up front.

One day, my mother sent me to Mr. Hale's store to buy six slices of bologna. I told Mr. Hale I needed six pounds! He asked me if I was sure that was the amount I needed, and I assured him that it was. He sliced, and the bologna started piling up. About halfway through the slicing, he glanced up at me and asked if we were having a party. I told him I didn't think so. He finished, and I charged the bologna to our account and took it home.

About ten minutes later, I was back at Mr. Hale's Grocery with six pounds of bologna in hand. Mr Hale and his daughters started laughing as I came into the store. He didn't have to slice bologna for quite a few days.

One of the most memorable things that ever happened to me at that little store had to do with the bins of fruit. They always looked so pretty to me. The apples were always polished, and the oranges always smelled so good. Occasionally I would reach up and get a grape and eat it if no one was looking. One day, though, I yielded to a much bigger temptation. I kept smelling those oranges, and they looked so pretty. I could almost taste one in my mouth. Finally, I took one. I slipped it out of the store, and ate it on the way home.

I don't know how my Mother knew I had been eating an orange. Maybe she smelled it on me as I came in. The point is, she knew. When she asked me where I got it, I told her. She was very upset with me and very sad. She talked to me for a long time about what I had done, and about how unhappy Jesus was also. Then she did the worst thing she could ever have done to me. She walked with me back to the store so I could tell Mr. Hale what I had done. I begged her not to do this. I promised I would never do it again. I begged and pleaded and cried, all to no avail. Off she marched with me trailing behind.

When we arrived at the store, she headed straight to the meat department. After she told Mr. Hale that I had something to tell him, she pushed me forward. Somehow, I managed to mumble what I had done and tell him I was sorry.

Mr. Hale came out from behind the meat counter in his big white apron, put his arm around my shoulder and steered me to the fruit bins at the front of the store. "The oranges are pretty, aren't they?" he asked. "I know you are sorry, and I know you won't do it again. Go ahead and pick out another one. I want you to have it."

I didn't know it then, but I had just been given one of the most valuable lessons on grace that I ever received. And Mr. Hale was right. I was sorry. I didn't even steal any more grapes from him!

The "New" Kitchen Floor

I am never quite satisfied with my walk with the Lord. I keep looking for that "feeling," and somehow it never comes. I am always hoping for a sense of being full of the Holy Spirit and empty of myself. I don't think I have ever even come close.

Recently, Jason pulled up three layers of old flooring in our kitchen and discovered beautiful pine wood floors under all those ugly layers. Getting to those pine floors was not easy. On top of the pine was a layer of linoleum with a green felt back that had been glued to the pine. A staple gun had been used about every four inches to hold the linoleum in place. On top of that layer was glued a piece of plywood, and on top of that was glued the linoleum which I had been looking at since we moved into the house. It looked awful. It was full of nicked places, and it was dull and lackluster from the years we had used it. After that last layer came up, I went to work. The floor was sticky from the glue, so my first job was to mop a small section at a time, and while it was still wet, to get down on my hands and knees and scrape the glue. It was backbreaking. I would mop a while and scrape a while. I was covered in glue, so if I had to walk out of the kitchen, I would take my shoes off on an old towel at the doorway. The kitchen is not large, but it probably took me five hours to get all that glue up. I mopped the floor again, and I don't think there was a muscle in my body that didn't hurt.

Then it was time to tackle all those staples. I had to stand up, grasp the staple with a pair of pliers and literally use my whole body to pull out the staple. I had only done a few when my neighbors Tom and Swannee appeared at the back door. "What are you doing?" they asked. I told them about the big project and how I was finally down to pulling out staples, but that it was slow-going. Tom said he would be right back and then disappeared. In a few minutes, he came back with a pair of vice grip pliers in his hand. He sat down cross-legged on the floor and methodically pulled one staple after the other out of the floor (bless you, Tom!). After all the staples were out, I swept and mopped one last time. The floor was ready at last for Jason to sand and apply the polyurethane finish. When he was finished, the floor looked like something you would see in a magazine! It was, to put it mildly, amazing! Tommy was gone that weekend and had no clue what we were doing! Imagine his surprise when he walked in the back door!

The first few days, I did absolutely nothing but enjoy my "new" floor and take great pains to avoid tracking in dirt or spilling anything on it. However, things do get dirty, messy, nicked and battered after a while. Things have to be maintained and cared for. Since that week, there have been some spills and messes. The first time I mopped my floor after the shiny new finish was down and dry, the water was hardly dirty at all. Though I was very careful at first about keeping it clean, it has now had everything from a gallon of tea to a whole plate of couscous spilled on it!

My life has been a lot like that old kitchen floor—nicked and scarred and dirty. I keep thinking that somewhere beneath all my nasty layers is a shiny, beautiful surface. I work and scrub and clean it up, and for a while it looks refinished and new. I try to keep myself clean and spotless, but I keep spilling things! When that happens, I have to let the Holy Spirit "clean me up." Many times in my life I have let myself go to the point that I just don't want anyone to even see me. It's a lot like being ashamed to let anyone in the back door when I haven't been keeping the kitchen floor clean. I'm thankful for floor-cleaning products, but I am even more grateful for the products that are available to keep me clean: God's Word, prayer, Tommy's sermons, my children, daughter-in-law and grandchildren who constantly challenge me to be better. Most of all, I'm glad the Lord keeps cleaning me up. Thank goodness for mops! Thank goodness for the cleansing blood of Jesus! Psalm 51:7 says, "Wash me and I shall be whiter than snow." I am sure that under all those nasty layers there is a beautiful person. I just have to let the Lord peel all that ugliness away and then keep mopping.

I just mopped. Come over and I'll fix you a cup of tea. It's okay if you spill it. It's easy to clean.

The Present

This was told to me by a friend over 20 years ago.

I was depressed. . .no. . .past depressed. I was almost
hopeless. It seemed nothing was going right. Quite
frankly, I wondered if it ever would. I tried to refrain from
self-pity and tried to be "cheery." I tried not thinking so
much about myself and more about other people. The more
I tried, though, the deeper I sank into my dark world of
nothingness and despair. I felt like the psalmist who cried,
"I am weary with my groaning; all the night I make my bed
to swim; I water my couch with my tears." *(Psalm 6:6)*
And again when he said, "How long wilt Thou forget me, O
Lord? For ever? How long wilt Thou hide Thy face from
me? How long shall I take counsel in my soul having
sorrow in my heart daily?" *(Psalm 13:1, 2)*

I was indeed cast down. It seemed I had abandoned all
hope. I did not even want to try anymore. As I sat in the
floor in my basement contemplating my plight and

wondering where to go from here, I heard a noise upstairs. Someone was running around in my house! Not only were they running, they were yelling! Terrified, I jumped up, for I was alone in the house. I ran for the stairs and as I reached them, I heard my girlfriend (in whom I had recently confided my feelings) calling my name.

"Come quickly! Come quickly!" she yelled. "I brought you a present!"

Instead of dashing madly up the stairs as I would have in times past, I just stood there rooted to the spot. I was in no mood for company, and I was in no mood for a present, but she was yelling again.

"Hurry up, hurry up! It'll be gone!"

Now, what in the world could get gone so fast? I wondered. But she was going to have the whole neighborhood over in a minute, so there was nothing for me to do but go.

As I reached the top of the stairs, she literally yanked me into the kitchen and dragged me across the floor, through the living room, and out the front door onto the porch. I glanced around, but didn't see any present.

"Look! Hurry before it goes away! I brought you a rainbow!"

There spread across the sky, in a brilliant array of red, orange, yellow, green, blue, indigo and violet, was my present! I wanted to reach out and pull it to me. Instead I reached out and pulled my friend to me.

"See!" she said. "No matter how dark things seem, God has set His bow in the cloud. *(Genesis 9:13)* It's His promise of hope, and there is always hope if you trust in Him. He will not forsake you!"

My friend says she still occasionally fights depression and despair, but because of the present her friend gave her, she knows that "Weeping may endure for a night, but joy cometh in the morning!"

—Psalm 30:5

The Race Is On

On the way to church today, traffic was backed up for miles. There is a race track nearby! In the summer there is a race almost every Sunday. Thousands throng to sit for hours in the hot sun and watch cars go around and around. Some camp out the night before to get a good seat. Some park two or three miles away and walk. Booths are set up to sell souvenirs. I have no idea how much the tickets are. These are loyal, dedicated fans.

When church lets out, things will just be reaching fever pitch at the track. I wonder if anyone there even wears a watch. If so, it will be for getting to the race on time—not for checking to see how much longer he or she has to sit. Of course, nobody sits the whole time. Excitement brings the crowd to its feet over and over throughout the race. The drivers are cheered. Hands clap, voices shout, and thousands of bodies visibly express how thrilled they are to be at the races.

I didn't have any trouble finding a parking place at church.
Just as well—I probably wouldn't come back if I had to
walk very far each week. I hope the preacher doesn't
preach on giving today. It irks me when he does that. After
all, my house payment is due this week. Lately we have
been straying quite a bit from the bulletin. Sometimes we
sing a song more than once, and many Sundays the
preacher is still preaching past twelve o'clock. Hasn't he
learned by now that people will only listen for so long until
their minds begin to wander?

It's the same with our Thursday night Bible study. After
all, our children have to go to school the next day, and
others have to go to work. Sometimes our praise and
worship will last over an hour! It's really enthusiastic, too.
I try to be reverent and calm, but we have some excitable
people who come. Just one prayer request opens the
floodgates. We even prayed for an hour one night! By the
time we got to our study, I was ready to leave. I got up
several times to check on the children and pour myself a
drink. That sort of relieved the monotony. No one even

noticed I was absent. They all had their eyes shut and were really "getting into it." Actually, I probably will not continue going to our Bible study much longer. Sunday morning is probably enough. One can get too much of this religion thing. People will think I'm a fanatic. That turns people off, and after all, I do want to win souls—it's my duty as a Christian.

> **As for me, I will hope continually and will praise Thee yet more and more. My mouth shall tell of Thy salvation all day long. . .I will also praise Thee with a harp. Even Thy truth, O my God; To Thee I will sing praises with the lyre, O Thou Holy One of Israel. My lips will shout for joy when I sing praises to Thee. And my soul which Thou hast redeemed. My tongue also will utter Thy righteousness all day long.**
>
> **—Psalm 71:14,15 & 22**

Reflection

It was a balmy summer night and I was five years old...

We didn't own a car in Fountain City because of the large transit system in Knoxville. We either rode the bus or walked. I loved to do both. I especially liked to walk with my mother or daddy. I remember feeling safe and protected with my tiny child's hand tucked safely into Mother's soft hand and Daddy's work-roughened hand. One particular evening, Mother and I had walked to the ice cream parlor several blocks from our home. Sometimes Mother would skip with me, and this was one of those times. I was happy and content. Nothing could harm me as long as I was with my Mother. We lingered a bit too long over our ice cream, so it was dark by the time we started home. That didn't bother us, though. We had walked that way so many times, we could just about close our eyes and find our way.

As we walked home that night hand-in-hand, something happened that is forever etched in my memory. It isn't a big thing, so I've often wondered why I've never forgotten it. I was so young and many things that happened to me then have long been forgotten. Why not this particular incident? I think I know.

As Mother and I walked along singing, laughing and swinging our hands, Mother suddenly tripped on the sidewalk and fell. I still remember how helpless I felt to stop her. It was as if she fell and hit the sidewalk in slow motion. I bent down to her to try to help, and I was sobbing as if I had been the one to fall. I felt myself wishing it had been me instead, because every time I fell, Mother would always make it better. I couldn't make it better for her, and I knew it. When I saw her knee all bloody and mangled from the rough concrete, I really started crying. Mothers aren't supposed to have scraped and bloody knees. She ended up comforting me as always. I sniffed and hiccuped all the way home.

Mother's knee healed and I went on being that happy, content child and put the incident our of my mind. . . temporarily. But it has come back again and again to me through the years. It became especially vivid when my mother lay dying with cancer. As I reflect, I believe I know why I never forgot the incident on the sidewalk, and why I never will. I didn't think mothers got hurt—only little girls. I didn't think mothers fell down—only little girls. I didn't think mothers bled and bruised—only little girls. And when little girls grow up and become mommies, too, they wish that mothers wouldn't die.

. . .but they do.

Reflections on a Child Leaving Home

This was written about 20 years ago.

I sent him off to school today. I did it once before, but he came home to me at the end of the day. This time, he is a hundred miles away. Before, I could not wait to gather his round, chubby, chalk-and-schoolroom-smelling body into my arms and hear his ramblings of the day's happenings. Now I can hardly wait to gather his tall, lanky, after-shave-smelling body and his laundry into my arms, and hear his ramblings of the week's happenings.

All these years my husband and I have been trying, with the Lord's help, to prepare our son to live in a world that doesn't seem to care a lot about the Lord, or anything that relates to Him. We feel he is ready. When we look at our son and talk to him, we see Jesus, but no one prepared us for life without our firstborn. Our youngest son is still home, and we are grateful for the joy, laughter and happiness he brings to us—but he and John thomas are so close that he was not prepared either. He has been sleeping in his brother's bed.

But I'm glad I am sad! How tragic it would be to not miss a child! How scary to send one away who isn't strong in his faith—who isn't deeply committed to his Lord!

I don't know what's ahead for my son, but "I know Whom I have believed and am persuaded that He is able to keep that which I have committed unto Him against that day."

—II Timothy 1:12

I sent him off to school today—committed to HIM.

Both my sons still love and serve the Lord.
Thank You, God!

The Ring

The book of Esther is a fascinating book, and one of my
favorites. On the surface, it appears to be full of amazing
coincidences. The name of God is not mentioned anywhere
in the book, and yet one can see the hand of God
throughout. Tommy says that reading Esther helps us see
that God arranges events and uses people.

The book of Esther begins with the king having a party,
which the king does quite often. He wants his queen,
Vashti, to come to the party and show his guests what a
beautiful woman she is. When she refuses, the king bans
her from the kingdom. He then starts to miss her. He may
even feel he has made a mistake. This is where Esther
enters the picture. The king decides to choose a new
queen. He is to choose from among several young girls
who are brought in from all over the kingdom. Esther is
among them. Hence the series of circumstances which
seem so coincidental.

Why, of all the beautiful women in Persia, did the King choose Esther to be his queen? Why did her Uncle Mordecai overhear a plot to kill the king and tell Esther, who told the king, thus saving his life? Why was it written in the history books? Why did the king invite Esther into his presence when he saw her in the court? Why was Esther hesitant to tell the king of the plot to kill the Jews the first time she tried? Why could the king not sleep that night after she tried to tell him? Why did he pick the history book to read that night that documented the account of Mordecai saving his life? Why had Haman built a 75-foot gallows in his back yard that same night, and why did the king choose to honor Mordecai the very day that Mordecai's enemy, Haman, was planning to hang him?

Coincidence? I don't think so.

The story I am about to tell you may not seem to have any relationship to Esther's story, but I believe it does.

Our preacher had preached on the tithe and giving. He

talked about robbing God and being too attached to things. It was a wonderfully convicting sermon, and I came away determined to work on several areas of my life. That night after I went to bed, I noticed that a small gold ring my husband had given me over twenty years ago was missing from my finger! I got very upset and started to cry—then I remembered the sermon. "All right, Lord," I thought. "You're testing me. I know it's just a 'thing,' and I'll try to push it out of my mind."

The day after the sermon and the loss of the ring, my husband and I went for a walk. On the walk, we found a "hacky sack" (a small, ball-shaped toy that you throw into the air, keeping it aloft by kicking it). We picked it up and took it home to our boys. When we got home, I stopped by John thomas's bedroom and showed him what we had found. We talked a while, and on the way out I laid it on a chest by his door and went to fix supper.

Later that night, I was lying in bed reading when Jason came up and stood by my bed. He held his thumb out and said, "Kiss my thumb." I did. "Kiss my finger," he said. I did. He did this with each finger, and I obliged. Finally he got to his pinky. I kissed it and he said, "Kiss it again." I started to kiss it, then stopped, looked and screamed! There on his pinky was my gold ring! *Where? How? When?*— the questions poured out.

Between my squeals, Jason told me the story. He had gone into his brother's room, saw the hacky sack, picked it up and started playing with it. He dropped it, and when it fell, it struck something on the floor. It was so tiny, he could hardly see it, but the light caught it and he bent over to pick it up. It was my ring!

Now, how does this relate to Esther's story? Why did I lose my ring the night of the sermon that had so convicted me not to let "things" rule my life? Why did my husband and I walk the route we did the next evening? Why was the hacky sack lying by the side of the road? Why were we on that side of the road when there is a sidewalk on the other side? Why did we pick it up? Why did I lay it where I did?

Why did my son pick it up when he did? Why did he drop
it where he did and pick it up again before I ran the vacuum
the next day?

I believe God is interested in all areas of our lives. I
believe He wanted to see if I really did want to change
some things in my life. I also believe, like a loving Father,
He wants to give us the desires of our hearts, and He knew
that the tiny ring had sentimental value.

I will never forget losing the ring, and I will never forget
that our Lord in His loving, caring, giving way gave it back
to me. Coincidence? I don't think so! God arranges events
and uses people. The book of Esther holds two famous
verses:

> **For if you remain completely silent at this time, relief
> and deliverance will arise for the Jews from another
> place, but you and your father's house will perish.
> Yet who knows whether you have come to the
> kingdom for such a time as this?** (4:14)

> **Go, gather all the Jews who are present in Shushan,
> and fast for me; neither eat nor drink for three days,
> night or day. My maids and I will fast likewise. And
> so I will go to the king, which is against the law: and
> if I perish, I perish!** (4:16)

All of us, if we are sensitive, can see the hand of God in our lives. We can see that the things that happen may not just be coincidences. If we open ourselves up to the leading of God and have the attitude of Esther that we will be used of God even if we perish, then with Mordecai we might one day be able to say, "I came to the kingdom for such a time as this!"

Visit johnthomasoaks.com *for information about Jt's musical version of Esther, STAR QUEEN!*

Say It with Flair!

I want to feel good about myself. If you like something I have done or said, say so—but say it with flair. Don't just say, "You did a good job!" or, "You fixed a nice meal," or, "You wrote a good story," or, "You drew a nice picture," or, "You look neat today," or, "You gave a lovely talk."

Instead say, "When you do a job, I can always depend on it to be done right, and you certainly haven't disappointed me."

Say, "I would rather eat your cooking than eat in the finest restaurant!"

Say, "Your stories always paint a picture," or, "Your pictures always tell a story!"

Say, "I am always proud to be with you, because you always look so wonderful. The way you dress seems to indicate that you care about yourself!"

Say, "I lose track of the time when you speak. You capture my attention and hold it until the end."

I'm not saying you should lie, but some of us are
unbearably dull with our compliments. No wonder many
of our children have such low self-esteem. When they
show us a scribbled piece of artwork, we mumble and
murmur, "Uh-huh—that's nice, Honey."
Instead try, "Oh, what a beautiful drawing! I want to frame
this and hang it up!" Then go and actually hang it up!
Encouragement and praise have made the difference
between someone who continues to draw stick figures all
his life and someone who has his work displayed in
galleries. It has made the difference between someone who
plays chopsticks all her life and someone who becomes a
great composer. It has made the difference in a shy retiring
woman who is afraid to read the minutes of her club and
Oprah Winfrey who at age three and a half was giving a
speech in church and heard the sisters telling her
grandmother, "That child is gifted!" And self-confident
Oprah says, "I was!"

Thank you, Fidge—you were the inspiration for this!

Second-Mile Attitude

What makes one teacher the school favorite and another the school UN-favorite? What makes one camp counselor loved by all and another despised? What makes one parent fun to be with and another fun to be without? What makes one worker do only what he is paid to do (and maybe a little less) and another do his job well (and perhaps a little more)? What makes one board member always negative about new ideas and suggestions and another always positive? What makes one mother put flowers in her home (especially ones brought to her by her children) and another feel it's too much bother? What makes one dad kiss, tickle, tumble and giggle with his children while another father is too busy? What makes one clerk in a department store smile and act pleasant and one frown and act like a grouch? I believe the answer is attitude. In the Sermon on the Mount, Jesus said:

> **But I say unto you, that ye resist not evil: but**
> **whosoever shall smite thee on thy right cheek, turn**

**to him the other also. And if any man will sue thee at
the law, and take away thy coat, let him have thy
cloak also.** *And whosoever shall compel thee to go a
mile, go with him twain.*

—Matthew 5:39-41, emphasis mine

If we develop this second-mile attitude, we and the people
whose lives we touch will naturally be happier. Lots of
things may not really be part of our job or assignment, and
perhaps no one else will know we have done something
extra. Regardless, if we want to be like Jesus we will go
the second mile.

How about it? Do people feel gratitude for your attitude?

Strawberry Shower Gel

Tommy and I were in "the Wal-mart" buying vitamins.
Even at Wal-mart they are rather expensive. As usual, our
funds seemed to be tighter in the summer, so we were
trying to be frugal and only get what we came for. As many
of you know, that is hard to do at "the Wal-mart" (this
should be said with a southern accent, with an emphasis on
the "Wal!"). While Tommy was picking out the vitamins, I
was browsing nearby in the health and beauty section (big
mistake!). I have this thing about good-smelling shower
soaps, and there are a lot out there right now, let me tell
you! I love the Bath and Body smell-good soaps, but since
they are definitely out of my price range, I go to Big Lots
or "the Wal-mart!" When Tommy walked up after picking
out the vitamins, I was looking at Strawberry Shower Gel.

"Whatcha got?" Tommy asked.

"Strawberry Shower Gel," I replied as I sat it back on the
shelf.

"How much is it?" he asked.

"$1.87," I answered.

"Do you want to get it?"

"Yes," I said, "but we can't afford it."

Tommy looked at me and said something I will never forget: "Life is too short not to have Strawberry shower gel!"

I love my husband for many, many reasons, but one of them is because of his Strawberry Shower Gel philosophy. That shower gel is gone now—all used up—but I will never forget buying it or using it. I smelled like strawberries for a while, but I will always be able to smell strawberries whether I have the gel or not. Every day smells sweet because of Tommy's presence in my life.

I have all and abound. I am full, having received from "Tommy". . .a sweet-smelling aroma. . .well pleasing to God.

—My paraphrase of Philippians 4:18

Surf's Up!

It was cold in East Tennessee last week, so we went to the beach to get warm. When we arrived, it was just as cold as it was back home! I wore a sweater almost the whole time! I sat on a blanket on the shore wrapped up in a beach coat. The boys and my husband went into the ocean, but it was just too cold for me. I waded at the edge a few times, and once my "funny" husband picked me up and carried me toward the water. As soon as I could get away from him, I ran back to the blanket. It was nice on the sand—calm and peaceful. I could watch the cold, huge and dangerous waves from a distance without experiencing them firsthand. I just didn't want to take the risk of freezing or getting knocked off my feet. I gathered shells, built sand castles, sat in the sun, watched all the action from the shore—but I never went into the ocean. When I returned home, I told everyone I had been to the ocean. I suppose they assumed I went into the water.

Tomorrow I'm going to church. . .

To Love, To Cherish and To Argue?

A word aptly spoken is like apples of gold in settings of silver.

—Proverbs 25:11

I have a growing concern about many couples who seem to be unhappily married today. I have repeatedly asked myself, "Why?" I also hear couples say, "You really have to work to have a good marriage!" After observing many of these couples, I've come to believe that "really working" isn't really working!

I realize there are countless books on marriage, and my husband and I have read many of them. There is a lot of good stuff in them, and we have put much of it into practice in our own marriage. We have also made good use of the best marriage manual of all—the Bible! Part of the problem is that many people won't read all the material that is available to them. Their lives are too busy (another reason many marriages are struggling). I have been thinking a lot lately about how to give people a condensed version of what it takes to have a happy marriage. I know people say there are no easy solutions or quick fixes, but I think there can be. Marriage is work, but it is also fun (or at least it should be!). Many have lost their first love like the church at Ephesus in the Revelation. Marriage has become not just work, but a drudgery!

I wanted to say just a brief word that could make a difference, if you will give it a chance. I asked my husband to tell me as briefly and simply as he could what he thinks can make marriage not just good or okay, but the best it can be. Then I will make my statement with the prayer and the hope that it will make a difference.

Tommy:

1. First and most important is to resolve to take the time and effort to read what God's word says to bring your life into conformity with what God has revealed about the

kind of person you ought to be (not your mate).

2. Sit down with a calendar and arrange regular times to spend with your husband/wife even if it's only five minutes a day over coffee. Establish rituals of togetherness.

3. Learn to seek and to give forgiveness. Walter Wanegrin says he thinks the number one marriage skill is not communication, but forgiveness. Of course, forgiveness affects communication.

Pat:

1. Eliminate the word "divorce" from your vocabulary.

2. Before you say or do anything, ask yourself how Jesus would handle the situation. Most of us know before we even open our mouths whether what we are about to say comes from Jesus or Satan.

3. Be fun to be around. Don't go around like you are carrying the weight of the world on your shoulders.

4. To reemphasize what Tommy said, concentrate on getting your life in line with the Word. Don't try to straighten out your partner.

One final word—when you read this, don't say, "Yes—but. . ."

Instead, say, "Yes—and!"

Follow that up with, "With prayer and God's help, I will!"

I really believe things can turn around for you today—that you and your marriage can be different.

Traditions

**One generation makes known
Your faithfulness to the next.**

—Isaiah 38:19

Every year at Christmas, Mother made Christmas pudding.
When Tommy and I were married three days before
Christmas over forty years ago, he had his first taste of
Mother's famous Christmas pudding. He loved it. All year
that first year, he begged me to make more Christmas
pudding. I told him no, because Christmas pudding only
tastes good at Christmas. Finally, the new bride gave in
and made Christmas pudding in July, even though it's near
impossible to find fresh coconut in July. We both agreed—
it just did not taste as good. Since then, we have only had
Christmas pudding at Christmas.

We have other traditions in our home. It has been said that
traditions are pegs on which to hang happy memories.

They are also pegs on which to hang a strong faith. When John thomas was two, we started about two months before Christmas reading the Christmas story from Luke 2. We read the first eighteen verses every night, and about the last ten days, John thomas could say it with us. We do it every year now so that Jason and John thomas will always remember it.

It is up to one generation to pass on the great truths of the Bible to the next. More than once in the Old Testament, we find God instructing parents to use many different means of teaching their faith to their children. It is very likely that more than one Hebrew child was taught the faith by what he saw on the walls of his home *(Deuteronomy 6:6-9)* or by what went on at a holiday festival *(Exodus 12, esp. verses 26-27)*.

If you do not have traditions in your family, why not start some this Christmas?

Up in a Swing

By the time I was six or seven, I knew this poem by Robert Louis Stevenson by heart. My mother would quote it to me as she pushed me in my swing. I have done the same for my grandchildren.

I always had a swing. At first, it was on the limb of the maple tree in our front yard. Every afternoon as Daddy waited on his ride to work, he would push me in my swing—never high enough to suit me, because he was always afraid I would get hurt—no matter what I was doing! When I was five, my little sister, Teresa was born. Daddy figured we both needed a swing, so he found three large pipes, welded them together and concreted them deep into the ground in our back yard. As we grew, my sister and I would swing together. Sometimes we would "race." sometimes we would synchronize. Sometimes we would hold hands, but the best times were when Mother or Daddy would push us. There was just something about the feel of their hands on our backs as we would shout, "Higher, Daddy! Higher, Mother!"

I remember how cool the air felt on a hot summer day and I remember watching lightning bugs and hearing the sounds of night coming on when I would swing at dusk. Most of all, I remember the love of a mother and daddy who thought a swing was an important thing for a child to have.

We no longer have our swings, but everywhere my sister has moved, the poles have been dug up and moved with her. She has one big swing on it now, but if you look up, you can see four holes where two little swings used to be.

> **How do you like to go up in a swing**
> **Up in the air so blue?**
> **Oh, I do think it the pleasantest thing**
> **Ever a child could do!**
>
> **Up in the air and over the wall,**
> **Till I can see so wide,**

Rivers and trees and cattle and all

Over the countryside—

Till I look down on the garden green,

Down on the roof so brown—

Up in the air I go flying again,

Up in the air and down!

—Robert Louis Stevenson

We DID promise you a Disney World. . .

. . .and we kept our promise! We had been saving our loose change in a jar for about three years. Tommy had been saving his frequent flier miles. Finally, just before Christmas this past year, we went to Disney World— Tommy, John thomas, Jason and me.

It was incredible! We could not have had more beautiful weather if we had put in a special order, and the Lord had said, "Okay—so be it!" The temperature was in the 70s in the day and the 60s at night. We left rain in Tennessee and came back to rain, but while we were in the Magic Kingdom, it truly was magical—not a cloud in the skies the whole time.

It was one of those dream vacations that came true. The favorite ride of the boys was the newest—Splash Mountain.

They must have ridden it seven or eight times, and each
time they would beg me to go. Each time I declined—
more emphatically every time they asked. They begged
and pleaded with me all week, but I refused to be swayed.
It was a roller coaster that ended in a headfirst drop over a
waterfall which everyone could see from a certain vantage
point in the park. Just watching terrified me. However, my
boys don't give up easily. "Come on, Mom, it's really not
that bad! There are so many cute things on the ride. The
only bad part is the part you saw at the end and it's over
before you know it. Even that isn't bad—it's really fun!
You'll be sorry if you don't do it. You'll always wonder
what it would have been like."

Finally, they wore me down and I decided to go on Splash
Mountain. *After all,* I thought, *how bad could it be? I
don't think anyone has ever been killed on it.*
"Okay," I said, "You've convinced me. I'll go."
Now that I had made up my mind, there was one small
problem. The lines were so long, we would have to wait an
hour or more to get in. The boys had just walked right in,

but now it was the weekend and the park had probably doubled or tripled its crowd. I had made up my mind, though, and I was going to ride Splash Mountain. After all, what's a trip to Disney World if you never get to ride Splash Mountain? Now, with as much determination as I had mustered not to ride, I was resolved to go for it.

For two days we kept going back to Splash Mountain, but the lines kept getting longer! Finally, on our last night, during the Christmas parade, we thought, *Everyone will surely be at the parade, so we can ride before we have to go back to Tennessee.* We literally ran through the park. The streets were so crowded with people waiting on the parade, I thought we'd never arrive. Finally, after what seemed like hours, we reached Splash Mountain. We couldn't believe it—the lines were longer than ever! So I left the Magic Kingdom, came back to Tennessee and never got to ride Splash Mountain!

What's my point? There are times in all of our lives when we miss opportunities if we don't take advantage of them when they arise. If we wait or drag our feet, we may not get another chance. The Bible teaches us this lesson repeatedly. The five foolish virgins in Matthew 25 missed the opportunity to go into the wedding with the bridegroom because they weren't ready. By the time they were ready, it was too late.

In Exodus 4, Moses kept giving God excuses why he couldn't speak. The Lord became angry with him and even asked him who made his mouth *(v.11)*. God said He would tell him what to say, but Moses evidently didn't trust Him enough, so God let Aaron do the speaking. Moses missed out on a great blessing.

In a moment of hunger, Esau failed to hold onto his birthright, and never got it back.

The children of Israel failed to advance into the Promised Land as God directed. Their decision, made in a brief period, cost them forty years of wandering in the wilderness.

I have had the experience of failing to speak to someone about the Lord, when deep in my heart I knew I should, and never getting the opportunity again.

Often we don't take advantage of spending time with our spouse or children, and when we finally get around to it, it's too late—our children are grown and gone, or our spouse is not interested anymore.

I am sending out a plea to all of you. If you ever get an opportunity to go to Disney World and the Magic Kingdom, I hope you have a wonderful time. I hope it's as perfect and magical as it was for me, but whatever you do, don't come home without riding Splash Mountain or you will, like I, always wonder what you missed.

This was written in 1994 shortly after Splash Mountain appeared in Disney World. A few years later, I was back in Disney World and finally rode Splash Mountain. Sometimes we actually do get a second chance!

What If You Only Have One Coat?

It was one of those bittersweet times that one wishes for, and when it comes it is over much too soon. It was a perfect, never-to-be-forgotten day. It was a day that I would reach back and grab hold of many times in the days to come. Each time, I would cling to it possessively, not wanting to ever let go. It was a blue and golden day— a magical day—a day that left no room for sadness. I did not know how beautiful the day would turn out when it started.

John thomas and Jason wanted to go fishing, and because their daddy would be out of town, I agreed to take them and two of their friends. We got up early and took our can of worms that Papaw had given us and headed for the lake. I was really feeling sort of ho-hum about the whole matter, but it was such a crisp fall day and the air was so pure and

clean-smelling that I was soon as excited as the boys.
Almost as soon as we had our lines in the water, the fish
started biting—beautiful bluegill! We pulled in one fish
after the other. It was almost as if nothing could go wrong.
It was like the whole world was laughing with us.

We had caught about fourteen fish when another little boy
arrived with his grandpa. He came up to me and asked if
he could have a worm because he had forgotten his. I was
very sympathetic, but explained that we had only brought a
few worms with us and after careful examination,
discovered that we only had one worm left. I told him I
was sorry I could not give him one since I only had one
left. He turned and walked away. Shortly after, I walked
up the path to get a drink. When I returned, John thomas
said, "Mom, Jason gave that little boy our worm."
"He did?" I replied. "How generous of him! I think I was
wrong, don't you, John thomas?"

In my mind, Jason had done a very noble thing, and
suddenly the day seemed even more golden than it had

before. The day had become permanently engraved on my mind. The incident would come to surface often in the days to come, and I would reflect time and again on the great lesson I had learned from my son. I thought about the scripture that says, "He that hath two coats, let him give to him that hath none." *(Luke 3:11)* I wondered—*what if a man only has one coat? If he sees someone in need, should he give his only coat?* Jason had.

The story doesn't end there. My beautiful, happy day was coming to an end. I told the boys we were going to have to be going soon, and I started gathering up our equipment. When I reached to pick up my empty worm can, I glanced inside at the dirt in the can. I blinked and looked again, this time more carefully. There, squirming in and out of the dirt in the can, was another worm!

Another Coat Story

Our oldest son John thomas and I were waiting at a bus stop one bitterly cold day when a young mother walked up with her baby. I glanced at her and noticed that she was wearing a rather thin, worn summer dress, and that her baby was wrapped in a very thin blanket. As they stood there shivering in the cold, all of a sudden (as if in slow motion), John thomas removed his coat, walked to the girl and handed it to her. "Here," he said. "You and your baby wrap up in this." Gratefully, the girl accepted the coat.

Suddenly it was not quite so cold outside. I was filled with such warmth and love for my son that I could no longer feel the cold.

Give generously, for your gifts will return to you later. Divide your gifts among many, for in the days ahead you yourself may need much help.

—Ecclesiastes 11:1 Living Bible

Whitewater

Dave Wheeler, a professor at Johnson Bible College, used to preach in Converse, Indiana. While he was there, he did a unique traveling week of camp. A group of senior high campers signed up for a week of camp and Dave and a group of counselors would load them into vans and drive to Upper East Tennessee to Milligan College for the first half of the week, and to Johnson Bible College for the second half. In the morning, they would have a study much like morning classes at camp and then head out for a different adventure each day. One day was rappelling, one day caving, another was spent hiking. Still another was a trip to an outdoor drama. At night they met back at the college for praise, worship and preaching. Tommy was asked to preach and John thomas and Jason were asked to lead praise and worship. Because I'm the Mom, I got to do everything they did, including my favorite event of the week—the day we went white water rafting! I was scared to death to go, but decided I wouldn't miss out like I did at

Splash Mountain *(See the Disney World story!).* So at age 53, forty teenagers, ten other adults and I strapped on helmets and life jackets, grabbed our paddles and climbed into a school bus for the half hour ride to the top of the Ocoee Dam, where the Olympic Kayaking Trials were held in 1996. All the way up the winding mountain road, we could see the Ocoee river rushing past us. *How could anyone survive this?* I thought to myself. *How can I expect to survive when Olympic champions will probably flip over and be injured?* I was determined to go, however, since I had come this far.

We finally got to the top of the mountain and were assigned our raft and our guide. Eight of us, including our guide, were to be in one raft. One of my first questions was, "Has anyone ever been killed?" The answer? Yes. One in the past eighteen years. Silently, I helped pick up our raft and walked to the edge of the river, all the time wondering to myself if I would be the second! I listened, probably more closely than anyone there, to all the instructions. I tried to mimic exactly how to sit, how to place my feet (tucked under the seat in front and back of me) and how to use my paddle. Our guide's name was Mark, and as we paddled around above the falls learning how to paddle forwards and backwards and how to break and where to place our paddle when we did break, I found myself concentrating on his instructions with everything in me. When we finally put in below the dam, I blocked out every other sound but the sound of my guide's voice and breathed a great sigh of relief that we didn't put in above the dam! As we approached our first whitewater rapids, he said, "If I don't lose you on this one, I won't lose you at all!" This was at the same time the scariest and the most reassuring thing I had ever heard. As he barked out instructions and as all of us worked together to get through the rapids, I concentrated so hard that we were through the rapids and on the other side before I knew it. My reaction? If that was the worst one and he didn't lose any of us, maybe—just maybe— I could make it to the end. As we went down the river that day, I found myself relaxing and enjoying the trip more and more. I even found myself saying, "Bring on the rapids! My guide can get us through anything!" and I really believed he could! As we floated and paddled and rode the rapids down the Ocoee River that day, I started looking at all the beauty around me—the tall mountains on each side, the huge rocks—and I started listening to the rushing water and the other sounds of nature all around me. I actually started to relax and enjoy the ride. But even as I found myself relaxing and becoming more aware of my surroundings, I kept listening for the voice of my guide. When he spoke, I blocked out everything else and concentrated on his voice. Because of him, we made it down the treacherous Ocoee River. It was hard, and there were some rough spots, but there were smooth spots, too. Our guide was there with us through all of it. He never left us alone—not one time. He didn't get out and swim when the river was calm and smooth. He stayed in the boat. After all, there could have been another rapid just ahead.

At the end of the trip, we all said it was worth it and that we would do it again, but I would never try to do it alone. I'd have to have Mark in the raft to guide us.

I'm on another journey. I'm scared. Others haven't made it—but I have the best guide on the trip.

WWGD?

No, that doesn't mean "What Would God Do?" (although that's a valid question and worthy of our consideration).

When Caleb and Gillian were at our house the other night, they wanted to watch The Addams Family. John thomas owns the first season. Of course the show is hilarious and completely absurd—or is it? As I sat and watched Gomez and Morticia interact, the thought came to me that the Addams family would be a great role model for any marriage, especially a struggling one. I told Tommy that it would be a great theme for his next marriage retreat! No matter what Morticia wants to do, Gomez supports her completely, as she does him. They are completely absorbed in each other and in their family. One gets the feeling that in this family, there is total love and commitment. If Morticia wants to join the Ladies Society (as she did in the episode we watched), Gomez is all for it, suggesting that she have them over for tea. When she starts worrying about getting the house in order and becomes frustrated because her "black" curtains weren't clean and how they would add so much to the decor, he is completely understanding and supportive. Another thing about this couple is their utter devotion and love for each other. All through the day, Gomez stops whatever else he is involved with and utters tender words of endearment to Morticia, calling her by her pet name—Tish. These words are spoken in the most romantic of languages—French! One gets the idea that Morticia is a blessed woman! They are also thoroughly caught up in their children's lives and in the lives of Grandma and Uncle Fester and their butler, Lurch. Even "thing" is not just a "thing," but an intricate part of this household.

The Bible speaks a lot about marriage and what all of us can do to make our marriage and family the way God intended. I guess Gomez and Morticia have been reading Ephesians 5! So the next time you are tempted to be hateful or cutting or spiteful toward your spouse, or simply tempted to just ignore any of your loved ones, just ask yourself, "WWGD?—What Would Gomez Do?"

Yard Stories

To some people, a yard is just a yard—but sometimes a yard is so much more. I know one woman who considers her yard a shrine. She sits by her window to make sure no children run barefoot in her grass in the summer or ride sleds on her hill in the winter. To others it is a playground, a ballroom, a jungle, a beach, a picnic ground or even a giant canvas waiting for a beautiful picture. I have two yard stories I would like to share with you.

There's a Hole In My Back Yard

Some people just stared at it in disbelief. Others were more aggressive and commented with remarks like, "That's going to be nothing but a mud hole," or, "When it rains, mud will wash right over to your house." Some were even more blunt: "I certainly wouldn't let my children do something like that!" Jason and two of his friends, Adam and Keith, had been digging and sweating over that hole for about two months. It had grown to a fairly good size. I had watched them work in the hot sun until they were wet with sweat. They had planned and schemed about that hole and measured its width and depth a dozen times, but I never heard them call it a hole. Most of the time it was a fort. It might have become a castle or a dugout or a foxhole, or if it did happen to rain enough, a moat! But it never was just a hole to them.

Yes, I have a hole in my back yard. Perhaps to some it is an eyesore. To others it is probably a nuisance. It may even depreciate the neighborhood! But in the eyes of my son, it is a wonderful, magical place. A place of adventure and excitement.

The hole in my yard may be filled in someday and when grass has been sown over it, no one will ever know it was there. But once a little boy full of wonder and joy is grown, he can never be made into a little boy again. I want to keep him a little boy as long as I can. And you know what? I may never fill in that hole. It kinda grows on you after a while. Perhaps it could even be a fish pond someday! It will never be just a hole.

A Love Story

It was a blistery hot and extremely humid July day. My husband was out of town for the week, and I knew when I got up that morning and looked outside that today would have to be the day. I had put it off long enough. I was going to have to mow the grass. Maybe that doesn't sound like such a big deal, but in upper east Tennessee, some of the hills in our yards would look like small mountains to those of you in the flat land. Ours is no exception. When we moved here it was decided I would not mow. The hills were so steep it might be dangerous. My husband wore baseball cleats to mow in! Danger or no danger, I marched outdoors to face the challenge.

I was not prepared for how hard it truly was. After several attempts, I got our twenty-year-old mower started (not the self-propelled kind) and began the long, arduous task of mowing our acre of yard. As I pushed, groaned and struggled up hills, looked forward to down hills and prayed for a breeze no matter how faint, I started grumbling to myself. *Why did we have to have such a large yard, and why did it have to be so hilly, and why did Tommy have to travel so much, and I'll bet I'm going to have a heat stroke!* On and on I walked and on and on I talked, feeling sorrier and sorrier for myself with each push of the mower. Finally, just when I thought I would collapse any minute, I looked up and there stood my twelve-year-old with a glass of water. "Want me to rest you, Mom?" he asked. "Dad lets me mow on the flat places." What welcome words! I gladly turned it over to him and walked over into the shade to cool off and drink my ice water.

After sitting a while, I began to notice that John thomas kept looking over at me and grinning. I didn't think too much about that, though. He was always grinning about something. However, I soon noticed that he wasn't following the normal mowing pattern. "Oh, well!" I thought. "I'm too tired to walk over and set him straight. As long as it's mowed, I don't guess it matters how it's done." So I sat and fanned and watched and drank my delicious ice water.

Finally, John thomas stopped mowing and yelled at me to come over. Slightly perturbed, I dragged myself to my feet, noticing he had missed a right sizable spot. When I reached him, he just stood there and grinned. I was beginning to get a little irritated at his cheerful attitude! I wanted everyone to be as miserable as I was! I opened my mouth to tell him he had missed a spot. Then I glanced down at the spot he had missed. There in the grass he had very carefully and meticulously mowed the shape of a heart! From that point on, I don't remember being hot or tired. My feet fairly flew and my heart sang. He and I finished the yard just as dusk began to creep over our newly mown lawn, and as the much-wished-for night breezes blew over me, I thanked God over and over for this precious gift of love—my son.

You Can Never Go Back

Someone once said, "You can never go back." They were very wise. I think all of us try, though, at some time or other. I did. Last night was my thirty-year high school class reunion. My class was very large—over three hundred. The school itself had over 1500. It was a school one could easily become lost in—only a number, or a face in a crowd. I was like that—partly because it was made up of many wealthy students and we were not very wealthy, and partly because I chose to be. Part of me wanted to be popular and well-liked, and I did try to be a friend, but part of me knew that there was a price to pay to be part of the "in" crowd. I was not willing to pay the price.

I went back last night mostly out of curiosity, but also to see a few old friends who were a lot like me in high school (or so I thought), only to find that they had finally broken over and become a part of that "in" crowd. They had finally decided to do what everyone else was doing. As I looked around the smoke-filled room, watched the

candlelight reflected in the cocktail glasses and heard some
of the language, I thought, "You can't go back—but some
of us try."